"If I had asked people they wanted they wou said faster horses."

Henry Ford

BMT Nigel Gee

For 30 years BMT has provided naval architecture and engineering to the world's most specialised vessels. We believe that looking to the future with new perspectives helps us deliver more innovative, creative and environmentally sustainable designs, today. Our reputation is built on results.

BMT proudly support Ben Ainslie Racing #BringTheCupHome

www.bmtyachts.com

WORKING TOGETHER TO BRING THE AMERICA'S CUP HOME

The America's Cup is one of the most prestigious of all sporting competitions. In the 164 years since the first race, only four nations have been victorious. I am delighted that the opening event in the 2017 America's Cup will take place here in the Solent where it all began in 1851. Thousands of people will have an unparalleled opportunity to discover a new passion for the oldest international trophy in sport.

Over the four days, Portsmouth will witness a spectacle of the talent, skill and determination of the world's best sailors as they vie for the right to take on the Defender for the 35th America's Cup. It is a hugely exciting time for sailing as the British Challenger, launching its campaign on home waters, seeks to bring the Cup home to Britain.

I feel very fortunate to have enjoyed sailing from a young age and know that it is a great way to build skills and confidence. As Royal Patron of the 1851 Trust, it is my hope that this world-class event will engage and inspire a new generation into sailing and the technology that surrounds it. The Trust aims to open a permanent Visitor Centre in Portsmouth as a showcase for the human endeavour, technical challenge and engineering excellence required to compete for the Cup.

Thank you for being part of the America's Cup World Series event in Portsmouth. Your support has helped to create a truly historic addition to the unique timeline of Portsmouth's maritime history.

Catherine.

WELCOME TO

Message from Sir Keith Mills, Chairman of The Louis Vuitton America's Cup World Series Portsmouth

It gives me great pleasure to welcome you to the first Louis Vuitton America's Cup World Series event in the UK and especially to Portsmouth. This event promises to deliver four days of amazing and incredible sporting action and entertainment to the widest possible audience.

The America's Cup is the oldest trophy in world sport with the first event taking place from Cowes, Isle of Wight in 1851. The Portsmouth event will be the first time a British America's Cup team (Land Rover BAR) will race in an official America's Cup event in UK waters since that first Race 164 years ago and so it's fantastic to be part of this historic moment. However, one disappointing fact remains: Britain has never won the America's Cup. In Land Rover BAR, we now have a British Challenge for the next America's Cup, the finals of which will be held in Bermuda in 2017. My passion and vision for the two Portsmouth events (2015 and 2016) is to capture the hearts of the nation, to encourage them to visit Portsmouth, watch the racing and get behind and support Land Rover BAR as they start their America's Cup journey.

It is really important to us that the event showcases Great Britain and Portsmouth and delivers profile and economic benefit to the country and city. We also want Land Rover BAR and America's Cup racing to inspire the next generation through our charity, 1851 Trust.

To host an event on this scale takes a huge amount of planning and organisation from a large number of partners. I would like to thank in particular the teams at Portsmouth City Council and the Royal Navy, without their incredible support the Louis Vuitton America's Cup World Series would simply not be taking place in Portsmouth.

For all of us in the UK, this is our opportunity to get behind Land Rover BAR and support the British team. I'm sure that the spectator and hospitality packages and event programme during the day and evening will cater for all and provide 'something for everyone'. The racing and entertainment, I promise you will be an unmissable and unforgettable experience...magnificant machines, with the world's greatest sailors, racing flat out.

LOUIS VUITTON
AMERICA'S CUP
WORLD SERIES
— PORTSMOUTH —

PORTSMOUTH

Message from Dr. Harvey Schiller, Commercial Commissioner, 35th America's Cup

The Louis Vuitton America's Cup World Series in Portsmouth is a perfect opening to the new America's Cup campaign. The home team, Land Rover BAR, is a model for the new America's Cup. The team exemplifies the best of sailing, from skipper and principal Sir Ben Ainslie, to CEO Martin Whitmarsh, to the facilities the team is constructing here in its new home on the Camber.

While Land Rover BAR will certainly enjoy the support of the home crowd, this is also an opportunity to cheer on whomever your favourite may be.

The competition will be fierce. All of the crews racing here are the best in the world, and each is as determined to win as Sir Ben. The racing should be spectacular as the AC45s have received an upgrade since the last time they raced. Now we will have flying 45s!

With a race course out on the Solent and a view that overlooks the Isle of Wight where the competition that would become the America's Cup was born, this is an event steeped in history.

We have strong, talented teams who are working collectively to create the best America's Cup ever, and our international broadcast partners and sponsors are bringing the race to viewers around the world.

On behalf of the America's Cup, I would like again, to extend a warm welcome to all to the Louis Vuitton America's Cup World Series Portsmouth.

Let the racing begin!

LOUIS VUITTON

AMERICA'S CUP
WORLD SERIES

AMERICA'S CUP
A LIFE LONG QUEST

Freedom, courage, skill
and competence:
the true spirit of Louis Vuitton.

2015 ▼ 2017
FROM PORTSMOUTH TO BERMUDA

The first Louis Vuitton America's
Cup World Series in Portsmouth
from July 23rd to 26th, 2015.

Follow the race on louisvuitton.com
and americascup.com

CONTENTS

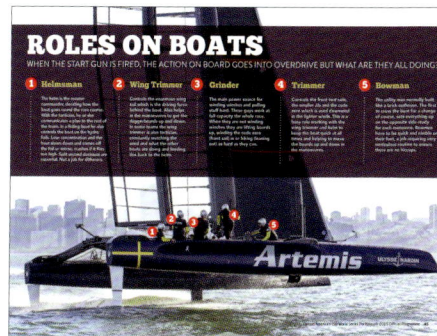

THE TEAMS

CONTENTS

MEET THE PUBLICATIONS TEAM

EVENT DIRECTOR AT LOUIS VUITTON AMERICA'S CUP WORLD SERIES PORTSMOUTH
Leslie Greenhalgh

EDITOR
Kate Laven

ART EDITORS
Gail Martin, Matt Tebbs, Chris Phillips

ASSISTANT ART EDITOR
Matt Alabaster

CIRCULATION MANAGER
Paul Smith

HEAD OF ADVERTISING
Mark Bloomfield

ADVERTISING SALES
Warren Lisk

CONTRIBUTORS
Leslie Greenhalgh, Charlotte Harmer, Carla Anselmi, Chris Draper, Bob Fisher, Edward Gorman, Julio Graham, Simon Greave, Sue Pelling, Matt Sheahan, Bernie Wilson, Dan Wilkinson, Peter Rusch.

THANKS TO
Alan Martin, Emma Kettle, Dave Thompson.

PHOTOGRAPHY
Gilles Martin-Raget, Sander Van Borch, Ian Roman, Mark Lloyd, Yoichi Yabe, John von Seeburg, Chris Cameron, Harry Kenney-Herbert, Shaun Roster.

PUBLISHED BY

PROGRAMME MASTER

www.programmemaster.com

For additional copies call
T 0207 121 5000 **E** enquiries@pml.media

Managing Director: Lee Berry

DESIGNED BY
Tobasgo Creative

PRINTED BY
Bishops Printers

YOUR WEEKEND PASS

If you came down to **Portsmouth today** thinking the Louis Vuitton America's Cup World Series is just about incredible boats involved in amazing action on the water, **you are in for a big surprise!**

Spandau Ballet

Red Arrows

The flying AC45s are amazing but they are just part of a mind-blowing sporting and entertainments package for the whole family that over four days is likely to put a super big smile on your face and leave a life-long impression.

Southsea Common will be Louis Vuitton America's Cup World Series Portsmouth buzz central from 10am to 5pm with opportunities in the Waterfront Festival Arena and the Fanzone Arena to see the boats and the incredible athletes who sail them, watch the action and listen to the commentary.

In between races, you can eat, drink, shop, dance, sing and if you want a better view, soar into the skies on a giant observation wheel. Get up close and personal to the amazing America's Cup trophy which will be paraded into the village on Thursday amid great pomp and circumstance.

Each day there will be a docking out show at the Historic Dockyard in the Royal Navy Base where boats will be hoisted by crane into the water. This will be followed by a parade of sail of the six boats as they head out to the race course where the action will be described by expert commentators to eliminate any confusion among those not familiar with sailing, especially families making their first trip of the school holidays.

Look out for the go faster Moths and the kite-surfers vying for speed on the Solent...and speed always means drama!

On Friday, the Red Arrows will lift our eyes skywards with a spectacular display of gravity defying stunts while the flying boats might also defy gravity on the water when the action commences in the first two practice races.

The serious business of scoring points starts on the Saturday with two races on a course that will be set on the day, depending on wind direction and weather. There will be two more races on **'Super Sunday'**

night with the booming Tony Hadley backed up by the two Kemps Gary and Martin with Steve Norman and John Keeble, recreating some new romance of old under the stars.

Scottish band **Wet Wet Wet** will be competing in the singalong stakes with their rendition of Love is All Around which was the UK's No 1 hit for 15 weeks back in 1994. They are warming up for a 17 date tour in 2016 so expect a good work out to their star-spangled collection of greatest hits.

Pop punk supergroup **McBusted**, famously formed from a merger of McFly and Busted in 2013, will belt out their catchy melodies and singalong choruses including their favourite Year 3000.

When Canadian pop star **Carly Rae Jepsen** hits the stage with her rendition of smash hit Call Me Maybe, it will set the festival rocking, showing exactly why it reached number one on the US Billboard list and topped the charts in 19 other countries including the UK where it was number one for four weeks.

Carly Rae Jepsen

Gunwharf Quays

McBusted

Wet Wet Wet

Royal Marines Band

On Friday, the Red Arrows will lift our eyes skywards with a spectacular display of gravity defying stunts while the flying boats might also defy gravity on the water when the action commences in the first two practice races.

counting for points followed by a spectacular prize-giving event. And when the boats have been packed away each day, the curtains roll back on the main stage to kick off 'Portsmouth Live' where a feast of local, national and international talent will fill the skies each night with their dazzling music.

For visitors who enjoy a mix of military marching and music making, the famous beating drums of the **Massed Bands of Her Majesty's Royal Marines** will lift the spirits with a medley of classical and contemporary tunes.

On Saturday night, more big guns hit town in 'Portsmouth Live' featuring British 80s band **Spandau Ballet** who have sold more than 25 million records. Hearing 'True' or 'Gold' ringing out across the Southsea air will make for a memorable

Portsmouth fans will be among the first in the world to hear songs from her brand new album EMOTION released last month which include hit single 'I Really Like You'.

This unique sporting and entertainment package was designed to place the Louis Vuitton America's Cup World Series in Portsmouth on an international stage to celebrate some formidable sailing and music talent in a world class venue.

Hopefully within a few years, there may be more celebrations here when Britain makes history by winning the America's Cup for the very first time.

YOUR WEEKEND PASS

GET CLOSE TO THE ACTION

While the entertainment will provide fun and festivities on the Portsmouth waterfront, the **Louis Vuitton America's Cup World Series Portsmouth** event is set to deliver an unprecedented four days of world class sport. Never before has a British America's Cup team raced in a British America's Cup event in Britain and never before has the Land Rover BAR team ventured out onto the race track against rival America's Cup teams. Not in Britain. Not anywhere.

OFFICIAL EVENT PARTNERS

OFFICIAL PARTNERS

Travis Perkins plc · Coors Light · BT Sport · 1851 TRUST EXPANDING YOUNG HORIZONS

STAKEHOLDERS

Portsmouth the great waterfront city · ROYAL NAVY

OFFICIAL SUPPORTERS

Gunwharf Quays PREMIUM RETAIL OUTLET · GOSPORT Borough Council · THE NATIONAL MUSEUM ROYAL NAVY · Portsmouth Historic Dockyard · RYA

MEDIA PARTNERS

BBC · BT Sport · heart 96-103 more music variety · The News · THE TIMES · THE SUNDAY TIMES · YACHTS &Yachting

OFFICIAL SUPPLIERS

aggreko · CLIPPER EVENTS · d2R DIRT2ROAD · HTP TRAINING TO A HIGHER LEVEL · Marine Events At the Helm of Quality Entertainment · PORTSMOUTH SAILING CLUB · SOLENT FORTS · SRC Solent Rib Charter · Sunsail EVENTS · Waitrose · WIGHTLINK PART OF ISLAND LIFE

OPERATIONAL PARTNERS

TEAMORIGIN EVENTS · ACTIVATE ACTIVATESWITCH.COM · EVENT360 ESTABLISHED 2002 · Into the blue · SPORTSWORLD · A Stone's Throw Event co. · TRAVEL PLACES

FANZONE ARENA

AMERICA'S CUP WORLD SERIES PORTSMOUTH

WATERFRONT FESTIVAL ARENA

AMERICA'S CUP WORLD SERIES PORTSMOUTH

RACE AREA

A SPORTING & ENTERTAINMENT SPECTACULAR

THE CORE FOCUS OF THE LOUIS VUITTON AMERICA'S CUP WORLD SERIES PORTSMOUTH WILL BE AROUND THE SPECTACULAR 'SOUTHSEA COMMON' AREA – A PERFECT SETTING FOR THE MAGNIFICENT 'RACE VILLAGE' AND THE BEST VANTAGE POINT FOR WATCHING ALL THE ACTION ON THE WATER

The theme of the event is 'something for everyone'. The WATERFRONT FESTIVAL ARENA takes up the majority of the Common and is a free to view area where spectators will find a full programme of family friendly activities.

A large hosted stage, big screens, local bands, food and beverage concessions, an array of exhibits and displays and a prime view of the on water action.

The ticketed FANZONE ARENA caters for those who want to immerse themselves in the world of America's Cup. An area dedicated to those who want to learn all about the sport, the sailors, the technology, the racing and how it all works. A staged programme throughout the day will feature the live racing and additional activities.

The Fanzone Arena also houses a ticketed grandstand for 1500 spectators and the amazing VIP HOSPITALITY WATERFRONT PAVILION for the truly best seats in the house.

If you have not already booked your space, go to www.ticketmaster.co.uk/acwsportsmouth

FOR FULL DETAILS OF THE DAILY PROGRAMME, THE SITE MAPS, THE RACING DETAILS AND TRAVEL INFORMATION, PLEASE TURN TO PAGES 104 – 114.

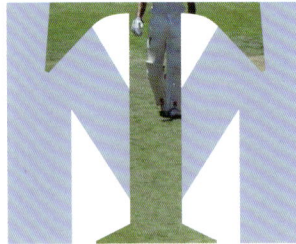

The RYS 100 Guineas Cup, crafted by Garrards
of London in 1851, became the America's Cup.

THE AULD MUG
THE OLDEST TROPHY IN INTERNATIONAL SPORT

The Royal Yacht Squadron bent over backwards to welcome a syndicate – mainly gambling folk - from the New York Yacht Club with their strange-looking boat *America* to join them for a race around the Isle of Wight as part of their annual regatta in 1851.

RYS had originally offered the Americans use of the Club's facilities in Cowes while they visited England where their schooner, with its avant-garde design quite unlike anything seen over here, would showcase US shipbuilding skills at Prince Albert's Great Exhibition.

But a face off had never been part of the plan until the 93ft boat, costing $30,000 (roughly £12 million in today's money) arrived in the Solent, having sped across the Atlantic in less than 18 days. According to a report in The Times, her speeds set the 'sparrow hawk among the pigeons' and 'old world' waters were suddenly muddied by 'new world' menace.

Officials at the RYS might not have known at the time but part of *America's* remit was to earn its owners sizeable sums in wagers, namely one-to-one matches with other boats.

There were no takers for such a match among Squadron members fearing humiliation but when the owners entered *America* in the RYS 100

Guineas Cup around the Isle of Wight on Friday August 22nd, they went out of their way – waiving long standing rules by opening it up to 'Clubs of all nations' - to welcome her into a 15- strong fleet, just to see what this extraordinary boat was capable of.

She won by a country mile having gained on the fleet when controversially, she cut a corner going inside a race marker while the rest of the fleet sailed round it. There was outrage until someone realised this was allowed in RYS's rewritten rules! More outrage ensued when a suspicious Squadron member went on board to check for propellers.

The grand RYS 100 Guineas Cup, crafted in silver by Garrards of London and standing a towering 68.6cm high, was carried back to the US and presented to the NYYC as a Challenge Cup to be perpetually awarded for 'friendly competition between foreign countries'. It was *America's* cup and that is how the competition became known though rarely in the 164 years since, has it been friendly.

This original event was marked by cutting edge technology, monumental budgets, rule changes, cheating allegations, massive wagers, intrigue, arrogance and some healthy controversy.

Little has changed.

QUESTS FOR BRITAIN'S GLORY

1851 -1890

It was almost 20 years before the British returned to the fray to avenge the defeat of the 100 RYS Guineas Cup 1851, the race around the Isle of Wight acknowledged as the original America's Cup competition.

Spurred on by Britain's defeat in that race, James Lloyd Ashbury fired the opening salvos by launching the first two British Challenges in 1870 and 1871 with his schooners Cambria and Livonia in New York. Both were unsuccessful.

Other leaders of British America's Cup challenges include the Earl of Dunraven in 1893 and 1895 in Valkyrie II and III. Lord Dunraven – Windham Thomas Wyndham-Quin, fourth Earl of Dunraven – was a larger than life character who played an active part in Irish politics and, for a while during the Franco-Prussian War of 1870, was the war reporter for the London Daily Telegraph.

ABOVE: Sir Thomas Lipton challenged for the America's Cup five times in succession between 1899 and 1930 with his boats 'Shamrock'

Britain's least celebrated performance in the history of the Cup was between 1886 and 1920 when not a single race win in eight attempts, was recorded. This period also saw the biggest loss in the history of the event when Lieutenant William Henn's gaff cutter Galatea lost by an embarrassing 29 minutes and eight seconds, in 1886.

1890-1934

Sir Thomas Lipton – grocery magnate and owner of Lipton tea – led more British America's Cup Challenges than anyone. Under the Royal Ulster Yacht Club flag, Lipton challenged five times with Shamrock I-V between and 1899 to 1930.

Two of them were William Fife designs including the 137ft Shamrock II, the longest Cup boat at the time. The final challenge for Lipton was in 1930 when he campaigned with a brand new class of boat, called the

J-Class, which was subsequently used in the design of five boats for the 1930 Cup in New York, all of them distinctive by their massive sail plan.

Lipton's boat Shamrock V designed by Charles Nicholson was beaten in four straight wins by Enterprise, another J-class boat skippered by American Harold Vanderbilt. The final race was a walkover when Shamrock V had to retire with a broken main halyard but the following year, after Lipton died, Shamrock was sold to wealthy British businessman Thomas Sopwith who used it as a template for his next J class boat Endeavour.

In 1934, Endeavour won the first two races against the American defender, Rainbow, and although she lost the series, it was the closest Britain has ever come to winning the America's Cup. Both Shamrock and Endeavour continue to race successfully today 85 years later.

Post-War

The first post-war challenge was a Royal Yacht Squadron syndicate led by Hugh Goodson in the 12-Metre Sceptre in 1958 but the defender Columbia was fast and won the Cup with four straight wins so America continued to rule the waves. Tony Boydon's 1964 Royal Thames Yacht Club challenge with Peter Scott at the helm of Sovereign, was the last time Britain progressed beyond the trials, to the America's Cup finals.

There have however, been a selection of British America's Cup campaigns since, including Boydon's Lionheart campaign in 1980 when Lawrie Smith helmed the radically-rigged Ian Howlett design. Smith also helmed Peter de Savary's Victory 83 challenge in 1983. After Graham Walker's White Crusader competed in Fremantle, Western Australia in 1987 and finished sixth of 13 in the Louis Vuitton Round Robins, it was 16 years before Britain challenged again.

OPPOSITE LEFT: A rare photograph of the schooner "America", winner of the 100 Guinea Cup In 1851 which became known as the America's Cup.

OPPOSITE MIDDLE: Charles Nicholson designed four British challengers between 1914 and 1937 including Shamrock IV but he never created a winning Cup design.

OPPOSITE RIGHT: Sir Keith Mills' TEAM ORIGIN America's Cup team was operational between 2007 and 2010.

ABOVE LEFT: Sir T.O.M. Sopwith at the helm of his J-Class 'Endeavour' in 1934.

ABOVE RIGHT: The restored J-Class 'Velsheda' still racing 82 years after she was built.

2000-2015

Peter Harrison's White Lightning/GBR Challenge for the 31st America's Cup in 2003 assembled a robust British team that included Olympic medallists Ian Walker and rower Greg Searle.

It was a strong challenge and the team reached the quarterfinals of the Louis Vuitton Cup Challenger Series but failed to qualify for the America's Cup Match. With lessons learned from the Harrison's £20 million GBR Challenge, Britain formed a brand new team in preparation for the 34th America's Cup in 2013, this time led by one of Britain's leading entrepreneurs Sir Keith Mills.

The Team Origin Sailing Team, representing Royal Thames Yacht Club, was one of the most professional British challenges in history and had the support of some of the world's best sailors including Sir Ben Ainslie and Iain Percy.

In 2010 however, a decision was made to withdraw from the challenge, when the Cup defenders Oracle controversially chose to switch from monohulls to multihulls for the next event in 2013.

It left those involved eager to find a solution to regenerate interest in a British America's Cup challenge and a year later, Ainslie, once again backed by Mills, launched his BAR campaign for the 2017 Cup.

CALLING ALL
ADVENTURERS
THE RACE OF YOUR LIFE
NO EXPERIENCE REQUIRED
YOU?
OPERATIONS
ANALYST
NURSE
DOCTOR
MARKETEER
ENGINEER
Join the only global yacht race crewed by people like you. No experience required
Sign up to the next series for a single leg, combine several or complete a full circumnavigation
APPLY NOW
clipperroundtheworld.com/apply
+44 (0) 2392 526000
CLIPPER
ROUND THE WORLD
17-18

BEN

Sir Ben Ainslie is the greatest Olympic sailor of all time. He has won four Olympic gold medals and one silver and is a multiple world and European champion in the Olympic classes in which he competed – Lasers and Finns.

The British sailing superstar is a champion match-racing sailor and enjoys the distinction of being the first British sailor to race on an America's Cup-winning yacht in over a century.

Ainslie played a key role as tactician aboard Oracle Team USA that helped the American defenders win the last Cup in San Francisco in one of the greatest sporting comebacks of all time.

Ainslie, 38, was born in Macclesfield in Cheshire but spent his early years in Cornwall where he learnt to sail on Falmouth's Carrick Roads first in Optimist dinghies, then Lasers.

Sailing was always in the family. Ben's father Roddy skippered a yacht in the first Whitbread Round the World Race and was a mentor to Ben from his earliest days.

Progressing up through the Royal Yachting Association youth system, Ainslie showed early on that he had tremendous natural talent. But what set him apart was his drive to get to the top.

This, he revealed in his 2009 autobiography "Close to the Wind," came from his determination to prove wrong the bullies at his school who picked on him because of a rash on his face caused by sunlight.

At his first Olympics at Savannah in 1996, aged just 19, Ainslie had to settle for silver for what turned out to be the first and last time against his rival in Lasers, Robert Scheidt of Brazil.

He got his revenge four years later on Sydney Harbour when he match-raced the Brazilian out of the last race to secure his first Olympic title.

In Athens in 2004 Ainslie won the first of his three Finn class gold medals despite being controversially disqualified in the second race.

On that occasion Ainslie demonstrated that he was never more dangerous than when the chips were down. Golds followed in China in 2008 and then at the London Olympics in 2012 when Ainslie thrilled his home crowds on Weymouth Bay with his fourth Olympic victory.

Ainslie has won numerous accolades, including ISAF World Sailor of the Year an unprecedented four times and he holds honorary degrees from three universities.

He has been appointed successively MBE (2001), OBE (2005) and CBE (2009) and was knighted in 2013.

He has been nominated for BBC Sports Personality of the Year twice in 2012 and 2013. He currently lives in London and married the sports broadcaster Georgie Thompson in December last year.

> Ainslie showed early on that he had tremendous natural talent. But what set him apart was his drive to get to the top.

Image courtesy of Land Rover BAR

The consensus among British Cup commentators is that Land Rover BAR is probably Britain's strongest campaign since 1851 due to the quality of people it has hired and the way it has gone about its preparation.

It was 164 years ago that the first America's Cup race was staged around the Isle of Wight and a British boat was beaten by the Americans.

Since then British syndicates have only lost while the Cup has been held by the Americans, the Australians, the New Zealanders and the Swiss.

The question now is whether Land Rover BAR is capable of finally claiming the oldest trophy in international sport.

The America's Cup is both a sailing race and a design race. It is also a hugely political event with every Cup cycle dominated by manoeuvring over the rules, the venue and the boat.

In order to do well, a Cup syndicate must tick all these boxes. It needs a world-class team of naval architects, engineers and analysts. It needs a world-class team of sailors and it needs a first class management team capable of playing the game with its rival challengers and the defenders.

The consensus among British Cup commentators is that Land Rover BAR is probably Britain's strongest campaign since 1851 due to the quality of people it has hired and the way it has gone about its preparation.

You have to go all the way back to Sir Thomas Sopwith's two Endeavour campaigns in the 1930s to find something comparable.

The aces in the pack for Land Rover BAR are Ainslie himself, the first Briton to sail on an America's Cup-winning boat for 110 years and a sailor who does not know how to lose.

Then there is a strong design team led by the hugely experienced Briton Andy Claughton.

He has surrounded himself by specialists from the marine and automotive worlds. These designers and sailors are backed by an impressive and passionate group of private investors, who were instrumental in getting the syndicate underway.

This is led by the likes of Sir Charles Dunstone of Carphone Warehouse and Sir Keith Mills, former deputy chairman of the London Olympic Organising Committee, who understand the sport of sailing and what is required.

Nothing is guaranteed in America's Cup racing. There are some formidable rival challengers and simple things, like the reliability of a small component on a hugely sophisticated boat, can let a team down.

But Land Rover BAR is making the right moves early in the cycle and if it stays on track it has every chance of giving ORACLE TEAM USA a run for its money in Bermuda in 2017.

LAND ROVER BAR

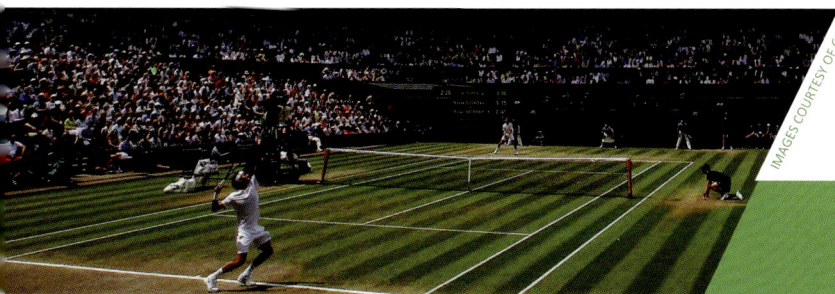

BRING THE CUP HOME

The Land Rover BAR team was launched in June 2014 and is widely regarded as Britain's best ever tilt at winning a trophy that has eluded British sailors and owners since the inaugural race round the Isle of Wight in 1851.

The ace up their sleeve is Ainslie himself, a remarkable sailor – perhaps the greatest alive. It is not just his sailing talents that infuse Land Rover BAR with credible Cup-winning potential, it is his long experience in the Cup game which has given him an understanding of the dynamics of winning and losing and what sort of team has a fighting chance in one of the world's most idiosyncratic sporting contests.

Ainslie has worked with some of the best challenger teams – including One World and Team New Zealand – and with the current defenders – Oracle Team USA. He knows what works and what doesn't. No surprise then that BAR is a relatively small team with carefully selected core members in design, management and sailing, all with proven experience and universal respect.

The team has a small sailing squad of just eight led by Ainslie himself and a much bigger design team of 20 led by the experienced British naval architect Andy Claughton.

Then there is a shore team and support staff of around 40 people combining experienced old hands with new young talent. Alongside all the human capital, the team has built a magnificent headquarters on Portsmouth's Camber Quay, which stands as a prominent statement of intent. It is there for the long-term and so is Land Rover BAR.

The America's Cup is *the* big-budget event in sailing with estimates for a competitive campaign, starting at around £80 million. Land Rover BAR has a strong group of private investors behind it that helped get the team off the ground and further corporate sponsorship has been secured. Everyone is confident the budget will be secured before the end of this year – a critical milestone in terms of its chances of success.

Ainslie has no qualms about stating his ambition. He is out to win and coming second will not do. "The goal is to win the America's Cup which we've never done and the tie-in with Portsmouth is very poignant because of our fantastic maritime history and heritage," he said.

"If we can go out and bring the America's Cup back after 164 years of never having won it, I think for all of us involved that is a huge motivation – to right that wrong if you like."

Among the key players are Ainslie himself on the sailing team, Claughton in the design studio and Martin Whitmarsh, the new Land Rover BAR CEO, who joined earlier this year and who previously ran the McLaren Formula One team.

And therein lies the second key theme in Land Rover BAR's approach. They have worked out that the control systems determining how finely the boat can be directed through manoeuvres will also determine where the Cup

WHEN SIR BEN AINSLIE GETS SERIOUS, EVERYONE ELSE NEEDS TO WATCH OUT AND SIR BEN IS SERIOUS ABOUT TRYING TO WIN THE AMERICA'S CUP FOR BRITAIN.

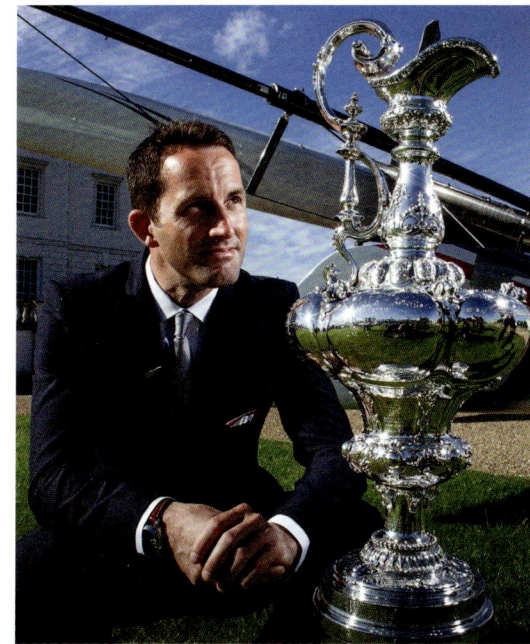

will be won and lost. Expertise in developing these systems lies not with Britain's maritime industry but the British motorsport sector that has dominated Formula One for decades so hiring Whitmarsh made a lot of sense in that context as does the tie-up between Land Rover BAR and Red Bull Advanced Technologies and the Red Bull star Formula One car designer, Adrian Newey.

"In the UK we have the core of the world's autosport industry with Formula One and other types of motorsport and we are really tapping into that expertise which is frankly streets ahead of naval architecture or maritime technology," said Ainslie.

Britain's most famous sailor is hoping the Portsmouth event will help spark national enthusiasm about what he and his team are trying to achieve.

It is striking that in addition to setting out to win the oldest trophy in international sport, Land Rover

BAR is also firmly committed to helping build Britain's marine industry base, encouraging children take up sailing and do their bit for Portsmouth. "It's vital that we work with the local community and that people come down and really get inspired by the event and the boats and the fact that the team is based in Portsmouth," said Ainslie.

For many years Ainslie raced small dinghies on his own to glory. Now he is commanding a crew on a twin-hulled rocket ship that can travel at more than 50mph.

But Britain's youngest sailing knight is loving the challenge he has set himself and the dream of victory is driving him on.

"Obviously it was a fantastic experience defending the Cup with ORACLE TEAM USA, and I learned a huge amount from that, but I don't think that would even come close to the feeling of winning it for Britain and bringing it back home," he said. "That would just be incredible."

OPPOSITE LEFT: Ben Ainslie has the America's Cup in his sights

OPPOSITE RIGHT: Land Rover BAR team puts new foiling AC45 through its paces in the Solent

BOTTOM LEFT: Martin Whitmarsh, CEO Land Rover BAR

TOP LEFT: Ben Ainslie holds America's Cup aloft in 2013 as winner with ORACLE TEAM USA

TOP RIGHT: Ainslie launches his Land Rover BAR campaign for 2017 America's Cup at Greenwich, London in January 2015

BOTTOM RIGHT: New state of the art BAR Racing HQ in Portsmouth

FRANCE

Groupama TEAM FRANCE

Team France's challenge to the 35th America's Cup was launched in late 2014 and is led by three of the most iconic and successful French sailors: Franck Cammas, Michel Desjoyeaux and Olivier de Kersauson, who have an incredible track record in both inshore, offshore and monohull, multihull international races. Despite having contested several times in the world's oldest sports trophy since the 70s, with teams managed by the famous inventor of the ballpoint Baron Marcel Bich, a French syndicate has never succeeded in taking it. Team France represents Paris based Yacht Club de France, founded in 1867, shortly after the 1st America's Cup.

ARNAUD PSAROFAGHIS

DATE OF BIRTH: 14.09.88
NATIONALITY: SWISS
SAILING CLUB: Société Nautique de Genève
STARTED SAILING: 6 years old
ROLE ON BOAT: Tactician

AMERICA'S CUP WORLD SERIES:
2011/2012: with Energy Team

The youngest member of the crew on Groupama 45 and a Swiss national, who was named "Male Sailor of the Year" at the Swiss Sailing Awards in 2014. Started sailing aged 6 on Lake Geneva and was racing 420s by the time he was 12 and Match Racing at 16 before settling on multihulls. A regular on the Extreme 40 circuit who competed in the ACWS in 2012 before becoming coach to the Red Bull Youth America's Cup team in 2013. Arnaud is a fine helmsman and an excellent tactician who knows the AC45 inside out having raced for two seasons with Loïck Peyron on Energy Team

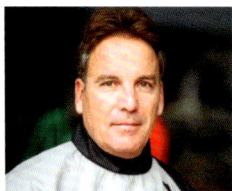

THIERRY FOUCHIER

DATE OF BIRTH: 14.03.66
NATIONALITY: FRA
SAILING CLUB: Yacht Club de la Pointe Rouge à Marseille
STARTED SAILING: 10 years old
ROLE ON BOAT: Wing Trimmer

AMERICA'S CUP:
1995: France America 95
2000: Sixième Sens
2007: Victory Challenge
2010: Winner of the 33rd America's Cup ORACLE TEAM USA
2013: Artemis

AMERICA'S CUP WORLD SERIES:
2011/2012 with Artemis

One of the few French sailors to have won the America's Cup. In 2010 in the 33rd edition at Valencia, he raced with Oracle Team USA on their wing sailed 113ft trimaran USA 17, having been involved in its design. His first America's Cup was in 1995 with France America 95 then in 1999-2000 raced with Sixieme Sens before joining Swedish Victory Challenge in 2007. In 2013 he was a member of Sweden's Artemis Racing for the 34th America's Cup. Teamed up with Cammas in 2003 and has been racing on Groupama ever since, including their Extreme 40 campaign in 2014. Known as "Fouch".

ARNAUD JARLEGAN

DATE OF BIRTH: 20.10.76
NATIONALITY: FRA
SAILING CLUB: SNO Nantes
STARTED SAILING: Aged 7
ROLE ON BOAT: Headsail Trimmer

AMERICA'S CUP:
NONE

AMERICA'S CUP WORLD SERIES:
2011/2012: with Energy Team

Another member of Cammas' prolific Groupama crew, Jarlegan switches effortlessly between one hull and two, having been crowned Formula 18 World Champion in 2010 after trying to win selection for Beijing Olympic Games in 2008 in the Tornado class. Has raced on Groupama's Extreme 40 catamaran and their M34 in the Tour de France à la Voile in 2013, which they won. Raced with Loïck Peyron on Energy Team on 2011/12 ACWS. "We need to increase our weight and power for the AC45 season," he says. "They are fast boats and very physically demanding. You need a good set of lungs."

DEVAN LE BIHAN

DATE OF BIRTH: 24.02.83
NATIONALITY: FRA
SAILING CLUB: Centre Nautique de Lorient
STARTED SAILING: 7 years old
ROLE ON BOAT: Bowman

AMERICA'S CUP:
NONE

AMERICA'S CUP WORLD SERIES:
2011/2012: with Energy Team

With a degree in plastic and composite materials, Devan Le Bihan is as at ease in a design office as he is on deck and as a result is one of the most sought after and popular sailors in international sailing. He won the Tour de France à la Voile twice with skippers Damien Iehl and Jimmy Pahun. In 2012 Devan sailed on the AC45 circuit with Loïck Peyron's Energy Team and returns in 2015 with Cammas. "The first race is likely to be tough. We're going to need to be able to quickly analyse and understand how it works. It'll be a tricky mission but that's how we like it."

FRANCK CAMMAS

DATE OF BIRTH: 22.12.72
NATIONALITY: FRA
BORN: Aix-en-Provence, France
SAILING CLUB: YCPR Yacht Club de la Pointe Rouge à Marseille
STARTED SAILING: 12 years old
ROLE ON BOAT:
Skipper and helmsman

AMERICA'S CUP:
2010: 33rd America's Cup with BMW ORACLE RACING
2013: 34th with Luna Rossa

Franck Cammas is a formidable talent and one of the most successful and respected sailors worldwide in offshore, inshore, single-handed, fully crewed, monohull and multihull racing. He won the single-handed Solitaire du Figaro at the age of 24 but took up multihulls a year later, winning five world championships on the 60' trimaran Groupama 2 and completing a series of ocean races and speed records, including the non-stop round-the-world Jules Verne Trophy on 103' trimaran Groupama 3. He shifted to offshore monohull racing to secure overall victory in the 2011–12 Volvo Ocean Race though his first taste of the America's Cup came a year earlier in 2010 when he joined USA's BMW ORACLE RACING. Three years later, he was called up by Italian syndicate Luna Rossa in Auckland as performance consultant on their AC 72. Cammas is currently campaigning a Nacra 17 catamaran for the Rio Olympics 2016. He is father of two girls, a trained concert pianist and an accomplished skier and cyclist.

'THIS WILL BE OUR FIRST TIME RACING AS TEAM FRANCE SO IT WILL BE DIFFICULT FOR US AGAINST TEAMS WHO HAVE BEEN TRAINING THERE FOR MONTHS WITH THEIR FLYING MULTIHULLS. BUT WE WILL DO OUR BEST TO BE AT THEIR LEVEL AND I AM SURE IT WILL BE THRILLING.'

GREAT BRITAIN

LAND ROVER *BAR*

To bring the America's Cup back to the UK where it all began in 1851 and become the first British syndicate to win the world's oldest trophy. That is the ambitious project behind the creation of Land Rover BAR led by the Sir Ben Ainslie, the most successful Olympic sailor of all time, who won the America's Cup in 2013 as tactician on board ORACLE TEAM USA. To achieve his aim, he has put together a group of very experienced and determined sailors as well as a high-profile design and management team, including former CEO at the McLaren Group, Martin Whitmarsh. The British challenge was launched in June 2014 in the presence of HRH The Duchess of Cambridge.

SIR BEN **AINSLIE**

DATE OF BIRTH: 05.02.77
NATIONALITY: GBR
BORN: Macclesfield
(grew up in Restronguet Cornwall)
SAILING CLUB: Royal Yacht Squadron
STARTED SAILING: Aged 8
ROLE ON BOAT: Helmsman

AMERICA'S CUP:

2013: Defender and Winner –
34th America's Cup ORACLE
TEAM USA
2007: Emirates Team New Zealand

OLYMPIC MEDALS:

Four golds (London 2012, Beijing
2008, Athens 2004, Sydney 2000)
and one silver (Atlanta 1996)

Sir Ben Ainslie is Britain's most successful sailor of all time and also the most successful Olympic sailor in history, having won medals at five consecutive Games from 1996 to 2012. He began sailing as a child with his family, a passion inherited from his father Roderick. By the age of 16, Ben was already a World Champion in the Laser Radial class and only three years later at Atlanta 1996, which were his first Olympic Games, he won his first medal, a silver in the Laser class.

Ben claimed the title of world's best after going on to win consecutive golds at the next four Games, in both the Laser and Finn classes. He raced his first America's Cup as tactician on board ETNZ in 2007 and in September 2013 fulfilled one of his boyhood dreams by winning the America's Cup with ORACLE TEAM USA, becoming the first Briton in 110 years to be part of a victorious Cup team. In January 2013, Ben was knighted, an event he describes as 'the proudest moment of my career'.

'THE SOLENT WAS WHERE THE AMERICA'S CUP FIRST STARTED BACK IN 1851 YET BRITAIN HAS NEVER WON IT. EVER SINCE I FIRST STARTED SAILING, AND SAW THE AMERICA'S CUP BOATS, I HAVE DREAMED OF WINNING THE AMERICA'S CUP FOR BRITAIN.'

LAND ROVER BAR

PAUL CAMPBELL-JAMES

DATE OF BIRTH: 04.04.83
NATIONALITY: GBR
BORN: Chichester
SAILING CLUB: Piddinghoe Pond
STARTED SAILING: Aged 5
ROLE ON BOAT: Tactician

AMERICA'S CUP:
2013: Runner up – Louis Vuitton Cup, Prada Luna Rossa Challenge, AC72

AMERICA'S CUP WORLD SERIES:
2012/13: Winner – Prada Luna Rossa Challenge

Paul Campbell-James, known as CJ, joined the sailing team last August, bringing a wealth of technical knowledge, mono and multi-hull racing experience. Campbell-James, whose father David was a British Olympic sailor, dominated the 2010 and 2011 Extreme Sailing Series (ESS), claiming both titles. He previously raced a 49er skiff with the British Sailing Team and had a successful match-racing career winning the British title four times. CJ was helmsman on Italy's Luna Rossa during the 2012/13 America's Cup World Series and reserve helmsman and performance analyst for the team's campaign in San Francisco 2013.

DAVID 'FREDDIE' CARR

DATE OF BIRTH: 15.02.82
NATIONALITY: GBR
BORN: Winchester
SAILING CLUB: Hayling Island Sailing Club
STARTED SAILING: Aged 3
ROLE ON BOAT: Strategist

AMERICA'S CUP:
2013: Runner up – Louis Vuitton Cup Prada Luna Rossa Challenge
2007: 5th – Louis Vuitton Cup, with Victory Challengee
2003: 7th – Louis Vuitton Cup, GBR Challenge

AMERICA'S CUP WORLD SERIES:
2012/13: Winner – Prada Luna Rossa Challenge

David 'Freddie' Carr is one of the most experienced America's Cup sailors in the team, having campaigned in three editions: 2003 with GBR Challenge, 2007 with Swedish flagged Victory Challenge and 2013 on Italian entry Prada Luna Rossa. He has an extensive multi-hull racing background, having competed in five ESS championships, winning in 2009 on Oman Air.

MATT CORNWELL

DATE OF BIRTH: 12.12.74
NATIONALITY: GBR
BORN: Coventry
SAILING CLUB: Royal Lymington
STARTED SAILING: Aged 6
ROLE ON BOAT: Bowman

AMERICA'S CUP:
2003: GBR Challenge
2007: Areva Challenge (FRA)

AMERICA'S CUP WORLD SERIES:
2012/13: Team Korea

Matt 'Catflap' Cornwell is an experienced sailor across monohull, multi-hull, fleet and match racing classes. He represented GBR Challenge in 2003 and France's Areva Challenge in 2007.

BLEDDYN MON

Talented young Welsh 49er sailor who is the latest addition to Land Rover BAR having come through Regional, Welsh, National Junior and National Youth Squads.

NICK HUTTON

DATE OF BIRTH: 02.03.82
NATIONALITY: GBR
BORN: Kingswear, Devon
SAILING CLUB: Royal Dart, Kingswear
STARTED SAILING: Aged 5
ROLE ON BOAT: Trimmer

AMERICA'S CUP:
2013: Runner up – Louis Vuitton Cup, Prada Luna Rossa Challenge

AMERICA'S CUP WORLD SERIES:
2012/13: Winner – Prada Luna Rossa Challenge

Devon-born Nick Hutton came up through the ranks of the RYA Youth programme and made his America's Cup debut in 2012 as bowman with the Italian entry Prada Luna Rossa alongside Land Rover BAR teammate David Carr. The pair enjoyed success together, winning the 2012/13 America's Cup World Series and finishing runners up in the 34th Louis Vuitton Cup. Nick has competed in six Extreme Sailing Series winning the 2010 title on The Wave, Muscat with Land Rover BAR teammate CJ. In 2014 he raced on the ESS circuit with J.P. Morgan BAR, as headsail trimmer.

JONO MACBETH

DATE OF BIRTH: 26.03.73
NATIONALITY: NZL
BORN: Castor Bay, Auckland, New Zealand
SAILING CLUB: Royal New Zealand
Started sailing: Aged 22
ROLE ON BOAT: Sailing Team Manager

AMERICA'S CUP:
2013: Louis Vuitton Cup, Artemis Racing
2007: Challenger and runner up 32nd America's Cup with Emirates Team New Zealand
2007: Winner – Louis Vuitton Cup with Emirates Team New Zealand
2003: Defender and runner up 31st America's Cup, Emirates Team New Zealand

AMERICA'S CUP WORLD SERIES:
2012/13: Artemis Racing

A three-times America's Cup winner, Kiwi Jonathan 'Jono' Macbeth is Land Rover BAR's Sailing Team Manager and most experienced America's Cup sailor. A former endurance athlete, Jono's Cup career started when he put on 25 kgs to join Team New Zealand as a grinder in 1997, then he successfully defended the 30th America's Cup in 2000.

ANDY McLEAN

DATE OF BIRTH: 06.09.79
NATIONALITY: NZL
BORN: Wellington, New Zealand
SAILING CLUB: Royal New Zealand Yacht Squadron
STARTED SAILING: Aged 5
ROLE ON BOAT: Sailing and design team liaison

AMERICA'S CUP:
2007: Challenger and runner up – 32nd America's Cup with Emirates Team New Zealand
2007: Winner – Louis Vuitton Cup with Emirates Team New Zealand
2003: Defender and runner up – 31st America's Cup, Emirates Team New Zealand

Kiwi Andy 'Animal' McLean is an experienced inshore and offshore racer, having campaigned three times for the America's Cup, twice for New Zealand and one with Sweden's Artemis. He has also competed in two editions of the round-the-world Volvo Ocean Race. In the 2012/13 America's Cup World Series, he joined Artemis Racing and as a qualified mechanical engineer, now plays the vital role of Land Rover BAR team's sailing and design team liaison.

GILES SCOTT

DATE OF BIRTH: 23.06.87
NATIONALITY: GBR
BORN: Huntingdon, Cambs
SAILING CLUB: Weymouth and Portland
STARTED SAILING: Aged 6
ROLE ON BOAT: Grinder

AMERICA'S CUP:
2013: Runner up – Louis Vuitton Cup, Prada Luna Rossa Challenge, AC72

AMERICA'S CUP WORLD SERIES:
2012: San Francisco on Team Korea
2013: Prada Luna Rossa Challenge

Like many future sailing stars, Giles Scott was sailing Optimists by the age of 6. He started racing his Finn Olympic single-handed dinghy in 2006 and five years later won both the 2011 European and World Championships. He remains the only man to have beaten Ben Ainslie to a major Finn title. Giles now represents Britain's gold medal hopes for the Rio Olympic Games 2016. His first experience in the America's Cup was with Team Korea, coming third at the San Francisco America's Cup World Series then he joined Italy's Luna Rossa for the 34th America's Cup.

The America's Cup
has a long tradition of excellence.
So do our official suppliers.

THANK YOU

Bermuda photography courtesy Gavin Howarth ©

AMERICA'S CUP
BERMUDA
2017

Butterfield

BF&M

FONDÉ EN 1743
MOËT & CHANDON
CHAMPAGNE
★

APPLEBY

pwc

JAPAN

SoftBank
Team Japan

SoftBank Team Japan is the latest challenger to the 35th America's Cup, having officially announced its bid in May 2015. Founded from an idea by Kazuhiko Sofuku, who previously sailed with Nippon Challenge during the 1999/2000 Louis Vuitton Cup, the syndicate will be led by newly appointed CEO and skipper Dean Barker from New Zealand, who comes with more than 15 years' experience and four America's Cup matches on board New Zealand's ETNZ. The team's main sponsor is SoftBank Corp and it will fly the colours of Kansai Yacht Club, one of the oldest and most active sailing clubs in the country.

JAPAN

WE CAN ALL BE CHAMPIONS

That's why we're supporting the 1851 Trust who are breaking down barriers and inspiring a new generation of diverse young people into sailing. **1851trust.org.uk**

'THESE FOILING AC45S ARE GOING TO BE A LOT OF FUN TO RACE. WE SAW THAT LAST TIME IN THE AMERICA'S CUP WORLD SERIES AND WITH THE NEW FOILING VERSION COMING ON STREAM, IT'S GOING TO BE EVEN MORE OF A CHALLENGE FOR US SAILORS ON THE WATER AND GREAT RACING TO WATCH FOR OUR FANS.'

DATE OF BIRTH: 18.04.72
NATIONALITY: NZL
BORN: Takapuna, New Zealand
SAILING CLUB: RNZYC
STARTED SAILING: Aged 5
ROLE ON BOAT: Skipper

AMERICA'S CUP:
1995: Winner with Team New Zealand
2000: Winner with Team New Zealand
2003: America's Cup finals with Team New Zealand
2007: Winner, Louis Vuitton Cup
2013: Winner, Louis Vuitton Cup

DEAN **BARKER**

Since 1995 when he was invited by Russell Coutts to train with Team New Zealand in San Diego, Dean Barker's name has been synonymous with the America's Cup. Just five years after making his debut, the 26 year-old Barker steered TNZ to victory, beating Italy's Prada Luna Rossa to become the youngest helmsman to win the world's most coveted trophy. He was back at the helm of TNZ in 2003, this time as skipper, but was beaten by Swiss syndicate Alinghi. He was then confirmed as skipper and helmsman for the 2007 Challenger series in Valencia where he led Emirates Team New Zealand to its second Louis Vuitton Cup victory though was again beaten by Alinghi in the America's Cup final. In 2013, Barker won his third Louis Vuitton Cup with victory over Prada Luna Rossa to qualify for the America's Cup final against ORACLE TEAM USA, which will be remembered as one of sport's greatest comebacks, ending with an incredible 9- 8 victory for the Americans having been 8-1 down.

CHRIS
DRAPER

DATE OF BIRTH: 20.03.78
NATIONALITY: GBR
BORN: Sheffield
SAILING CLUB: Stokes Bay
STARTED SAILING: Aged 7
ROLE ON BOAT: Helmsman

AMERICA'S CUP:
2013: Louis Vuitton Cup finals

AMERICA'S CUP WORLD SERIES:
2011: Team Korea
2012: Luna Rossa Piranha
2013: Luna Rossa

Chris Draper started sailing on an Optimist aged 7, and came through the RYA Youth programme to win a silver medal at the 1996 Youth worlds on a 420. In Athens 2004, he won an Olympic silver medal in the 49er double-handed dinghy, after having previously won two Worlds and three European titles. In 2009 he topped the Extreme Sailing Series overall rankings and four years later, became the first British sailor to helm a boat in the Louis Vuitton Cup, steering Italy's Luna Rossa during the 34th America's Cup Challenger. One of Britain's most talented helms.

KAZUHIKO
SOFUKU

DATE OF BIRTH: 25.11.65
NATIONALITY: JPN
BORN: Niigata Japan
SAILING CLUB: Kansai Yacht Club
STARTED SAILING: Aged 20
ROLE ON BOAT: Bowman

AMERICA'S CUP:
1995, 2000, 2003, 2007

Sofuku, aka "Fuku", made his America's Cup debut in 2000 as bowman on Nippon Challenge during the 1999-2000 Louis Vuitton Cup challenger series. Since then he made a career at the highest international level, taking part in a total of 4 America's Cups and winning World Match Race Championship twice. He joined USA's One World then BMW Oracle Racing for the 32nd America's Cup in Valencia. His aim is to help build a new generation of Japanese top level sailors.

JEREMY
LOMAS

DATE OF BIRTH: 06.02.72
NATIONALITY: NZL
BORN: Auckland
SAILING CLUB: RNZYS
STARTED SAILING: Aged 6
ROLE ON BOAT: Bowman

AMERICA'S CUP:
2000, 2003, 2007 and **2013** on Emirates Team New Zeland

AMERICA'S CUP WORLD SERIES:
2011, 2012, 2013 with Emirates Team New Zeland

Jeremy Lomas sailed the 1997–98 Whitbread and since then completed four America's Cup campaigns with Emirates Team New Zealand. He raced the AC72 at San Francisco in 2013 and through 2014 managed and sailed the team's Extreme Sailing series campaign. A regular competitor on the international grand prix and match racing circuits.

DEREK
SAWARD

DATE OF BIRTH: 10.07.81
NATIONALITY: NZL
BORN: New Zealand
SAILING CLUB: RNZYS
STARTED SAILING: Aged 8
ROLE ON BOAT: Grinder / Bow

AMERICA'S CUP:
2013: Emirates Team New Zealand

AMERICA'S CUP WORLD SERIES:
2012-2013:
Emirates Team New Zealand

Derek Saward was a member of Emirates Team New Zealand's AC72 sailing team at the 34th America's Cup in San Francisco having joined the team full-time in 2011. He had earned his spurs with them a year before when he sailed in two of the Louis Vuitton Trophy events. Derek has twice set the Transpac record from Hawaii to Japan and raced four seasons in the highly competitive RC44 circuit and is currently with the 52 Super Series.

TOP: Japan's Nippon Challenge reached the semi-finals of the Louis Vuitton Cup in 1995 on JPN 41
BOTTOM: 2000 on JPN 52

Our customers love to sail. Some, however, prefer to fly.

The Power to Perform

When you want to take sailing performance to new heights, work with someone who's been there. Contact your North representative to discover how we can make your boat fly.

North Sails UK (Head Office) +44 (0)23 9252 5588   **Ireland** +35 32120 61769   **Belgium** +32 (0)3 325 67 20   **Holland** +31 (0)36 546 0190

www.northsails.com   San Francisco Oracle Team USA media photo.

ROLES ON BOATS

WHEN THE START GUN IS FIRED, THE ACTION ON BOARD GOES INTO OVERDRIVE BUT WHAT ARE THEY ALL DOING?

1 Helmsman

The helm is the master-commander, deciding how the boat goes round the race course. With the tactician, he or she communicates a plan to the rest of the team. In a foiling boat he also controls the boat on the hydro foils. Lose concentration and the boat slows down and comes off the foil or worse, crashes if it flies too high. Split second decisions are essential. Not a job for ditherers.

2 Wing Trimmer

Controls the enormous wing sail which is the driving force behind the boat. Also helps in the manoeuvres to get the daggerboards up and down. In some teams the wing trimmer is also tactician, constantly watching the wind and what the other boats are doing and feeding this back to the helm.

3 Grinder

The main power source for winding winches and pulling stuff hard. These guys work at full capacity the whole race. When they are not winding winches they are lifting boards up, winding the code zero (front sail) in or hiking (leaning out) as hard as they can.

4 Trimmer

Controls the front two sails, the smaller Jib and the code zero which is used downwind in the lighter winds. This is a busy role working with the wing trimmer and helm to keep the boat quick at all times and helping to move the boards up and down in the manoeuvres.

5 Bowman

The utility man normally built like a brick outhouse. The first to cross the boat for a change of course, sets everything up on the opposite side ready for each manouvre. Bowmen have to be quick and nimble on their feet, a job requiring very meticulous routine to ensure there are no hiccups.

AN EVER CHANGING STORY

The America's Cup, the oldest international sport trophy, is a contest like no other.

Whoever claims the Auld Mug wins the right to decide the rules for the next contest such as what type of boats, when they should race and where.

This naturally makes the defender virtually unbeatable but odd as it may sound, this quirky tradition has been universally accepted and painstakingly preserved.

After they won the America's Cup in 1851, the Americans controlled it for 132 long years, fending off 24 challenges in the US before the Australians famously wrestled it from their clutches in 1983 at their seventh attempt.

Since then, the Cup has been won twice by New Zealand in 1995 and 2000 and once by Switzerland in 2003 though the Americans have been ruthless in their pursuit of the 'Auld Mug' and are the current holders with a campaign funded directly by the world's fifth richest man Larry Ellison.

TOP LEFT: Stars & Stripes (USA) reclaims Auld Mug, beating Kookaburra III (AUS) in 1987 America's Cup final Fremantle

TOP RIGHT: ORACLE TEAM USA retains America's Cup in 2013 beating Emirates Team New Zealand in finals

BELOW: Russell Coutts' NZ skipper turned America's Cup visionary.

Photo credit: Guillain Greiner

From the start, the America's Cup has pushed technological boundaries in boat and systems design and hired the very best sailors money can buy. Some of the wealthiest men in history have spent fortunes buying them, sometimes successfully, more often not.

They set out first to win the right to challenge the Defender in a series comprising many rounds of two boat matches that can take weeks to decide. The winning Challenger then goes head to head with the Defender in the Americas Cup finals.

Traditionally, racing was staged miles offshore so the thrill of live action was lost on all but committed sailing fans and wealthy racer chasers. In recent years, up to £20 million was invested each time on television coverage

But the game changed completely in 2013. A new racing circuit, the Extreme Sailing Series, had proved successful in drawing large crowds with a fleet of high performance catamarans hurtling around small race courses just yards from the shore.

The format was immediately adopted by Ellison who recognised the need to modernise the event. In came the electrifyingly fast catamarans and a new race course that swept the boats under the noses of astonished spectators on the beach. Television budgets soared to £200 million.

A superb sporting come-back story in San Francisco presented on television with never before seen graphics and revolutionary new camera equipment finally made sailing understandable to households the world over.

The America's Cup was reinvented for the Facebook generation and although traditionalists would disagree, is arguably in better shape now than it has ever been.

SAN FRANCISCO 2013
A SPORTING REVOLUTION

California based journalist Bernie Wilson recalls 2013 when the 34th America's Cup show rolled into town

Sailing had never seen anything like this before and neither had the sporting world.

The America's Cup swept fully into the 21st century in 2013, when Oracle Team USA, led by Jimmy Spithill and Britain's own Sir Ben Ainslie, overcame an eight-point deficit at match point to successfully defend the oldest trophy in international sport.

A summer that started with the tragic death of British sailing star Andrew 'Bart' Simpson in a training accident ended with Oracle's astonishing 9-8 win against Emirates Team New Zealand.

It was the longest, fastest and wildest America's Cup ever. A real white-knuckle ride on San Francisco Bay.

Starting in a hole due to penalties for illegally modifying boats in warm-up regattas, it took a deep resolve for

BOTTOM LEFT: Game changers: the new AC72s

BOTTOM RIGHT: ORACLE TEAM USA v Emirates Team New Zealand in the spectacular final of the 34th America's Cup on San Francisco Bay

ABOVE: Jimmy Spithill kisses the Auld Mug

the Oracle boys to continue to improve their foiling and upwind sailing during a thrilling eight-race winning streak.

All the while, they knew another loss would send the Auld Mug packing for Auckland.

The comeback was considered by many to be the greatest ever in sporting history.

"I'm going to rank it No. 1. We never gave up," Spithill said.

The TV images beamed around the world were spectacular as the boats circled a course bordered by the Golden Gate Bridge, Alcatraz Island and the city front.

It was the first time the America's Cup was contested inshore, making it accessible to spectators in a stadium-like setting.

The boats themselves were mind-bending - 72-foot, space-age catamarans that lifted out of the water on hydrofoils to skim above the waves faster than the speed limit on the Golden Gate Bridge.

The catamarans, powered by a mainsail that looked like a jetliner's wing, were difficult to tame. There were heart stopping moments, for sure, including when the Kiwis lifted dangerously onto one hull and hung in the air for five seconds, seemingly about to tip over before the sailors regained control.

Oracle's sailors had their hearts in their mouths in race 13, when the Kiwis were just minutes away from winning the America's Cup on a foggy, fluky day. But then, the time limit expired.

The Americans had escaped elimination, and capitalised.

For the rest of the regatta, they sailed with no margin for error in a new class of boats that had a learning curve that was almost straight up.

"There's nothing like going all in," Spithill said. "I'm so proud of the boys. They didn't flinch."

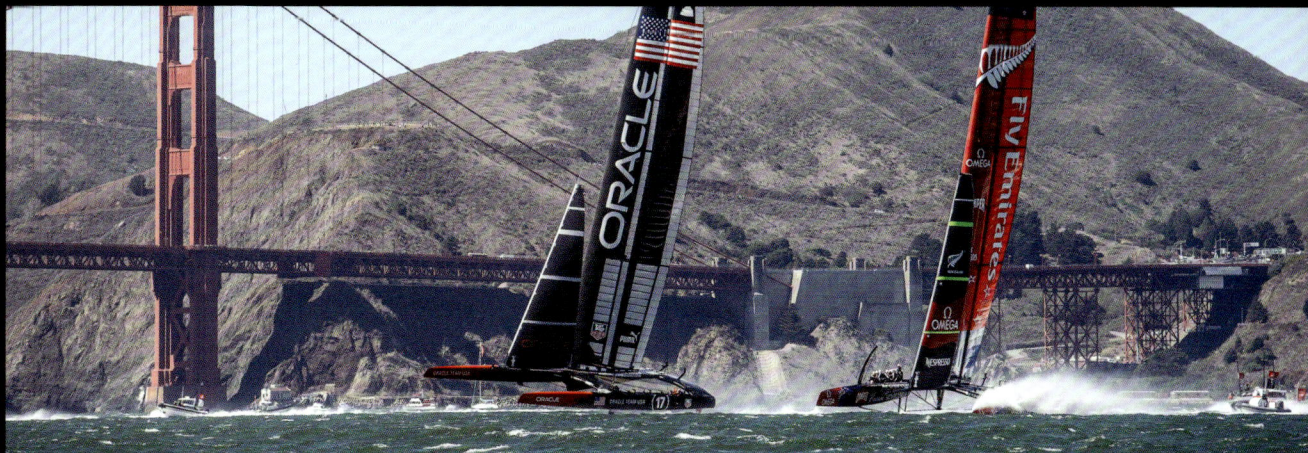

TECHNICAL AREA (ROYAL NAVY / HISTORIC DOCKYARD)

1. FRENCH TEAM BASE
2. NZL TEAM BASE
3. SWEDISH TEAM BASE
4. JAPANESE TEAM BASE
5. USA TEAM BASE
6. CRANE / HOIST
7. ACEA / ACRM OFFICE
8. GIANT SPECTATOR SCREEN
9. B.A.R MERCHANDISE & PROGRAMMES
10. INFO BRANDING

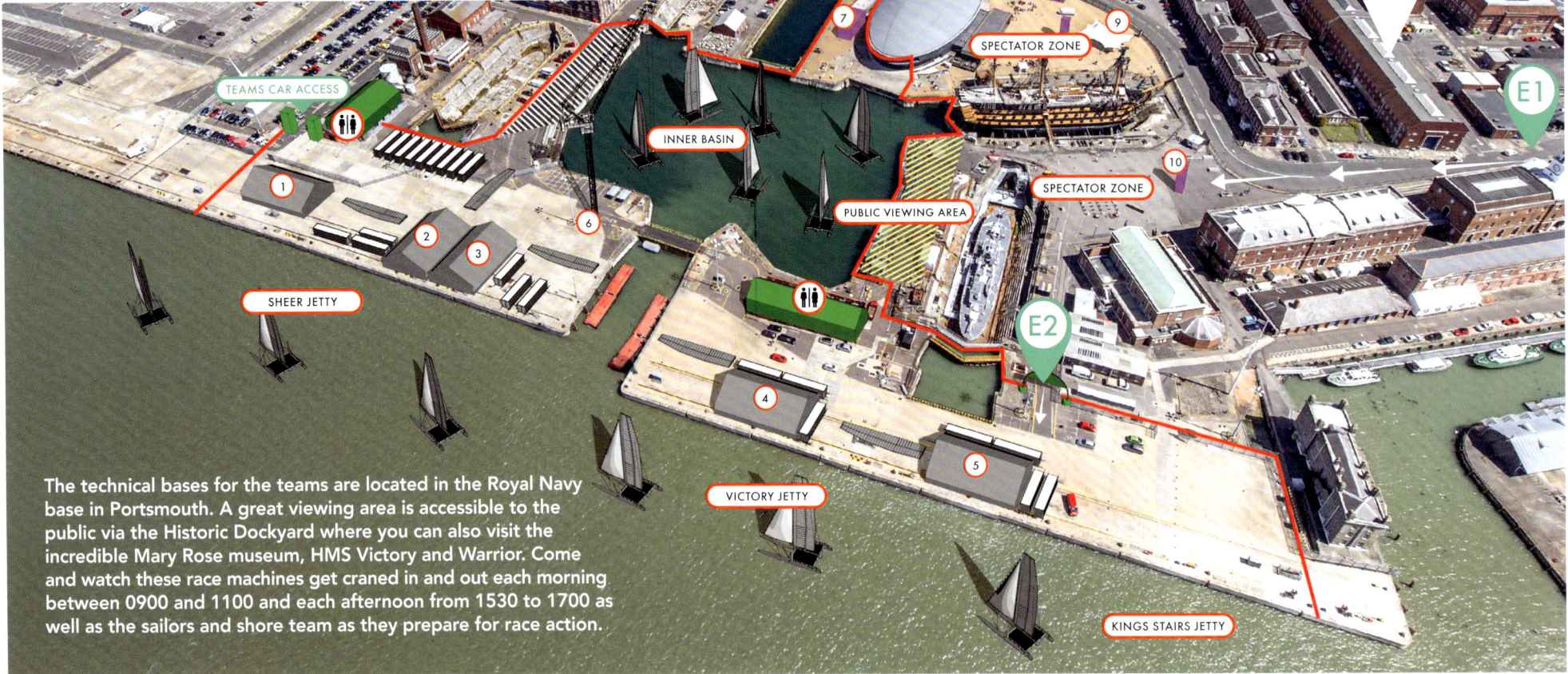

ENTRANCES / EXITS

TOILETS

MEDICAL CENTRE

LOUIS VUITTON

AMERICA'S CUP
WORLD SERIES
—PORTSMOUTH—

TEAMS CAR ACCESS

SPECTATOR ZONE

INNER BASIN

SPECTATOR ZONE

PUBLIC VIEWING AREA

SHEER JETTY

E1

E2

VICTORY JETTY

KINGS STAIRS JETTY

The technical bases for the teams are located in the Royal Navy base in Portsmouth. A great viewing area is accessible to the public via the Historic Dockyard where you can also visit the incredible Mary Rose museum, HMS Victory and Warrior. Come and watch these race machines get craned in and out each morning between 0900 and 1100 and each afternoon from 1530 to 1700 as well as the sailors and shore team as they prepare for race action.

 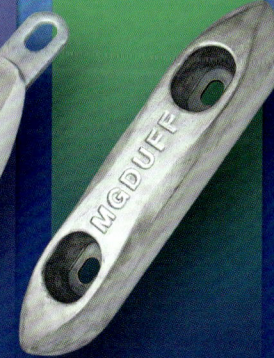 

FORMULA ONE FOILS

Martin Whitmarsh, CEO, Land Rover BAR

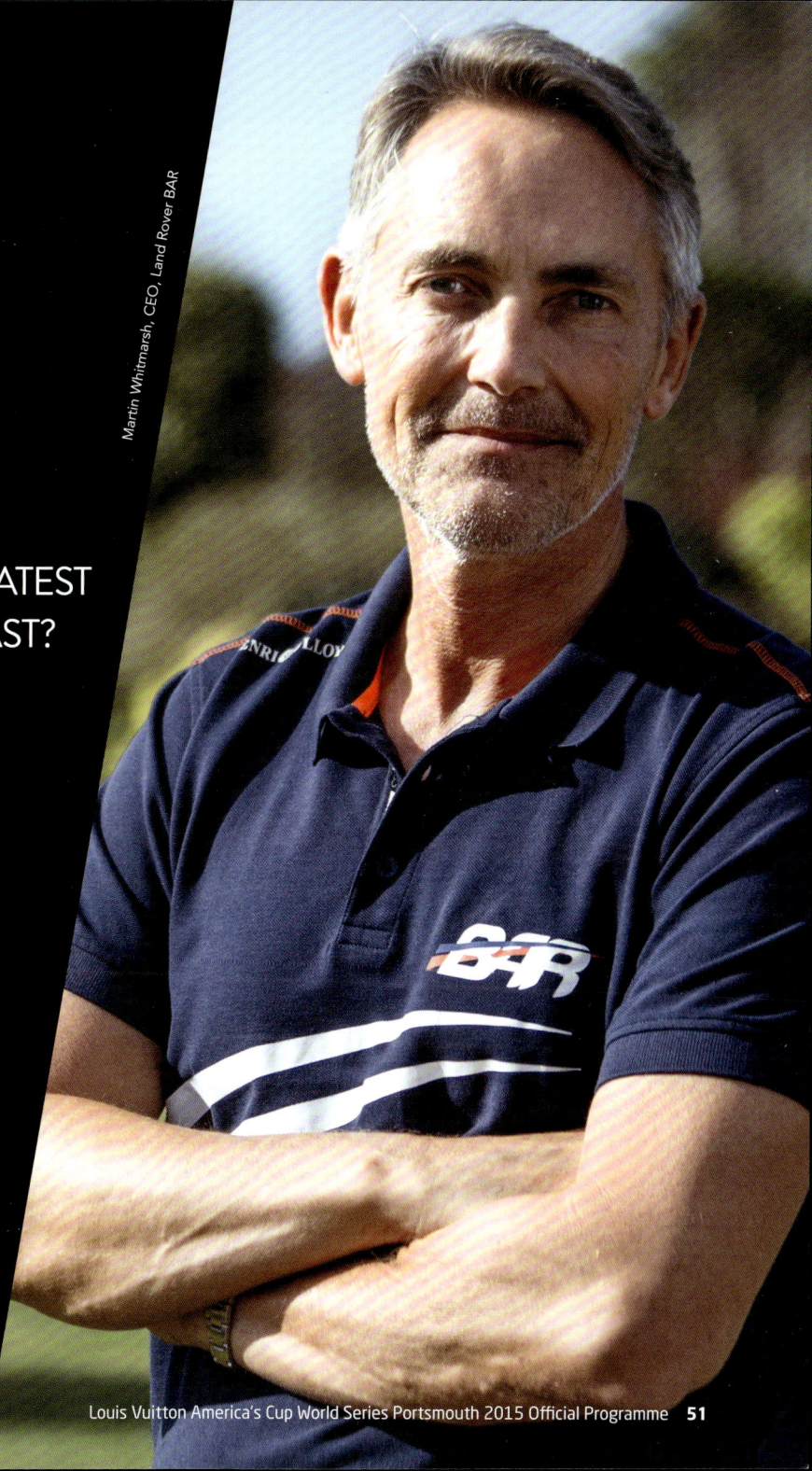

THERE IS NOTHING NEW IN HYDROFOILS, BUT HOW COME THE LATEST GENERATION OF AMERICA'S CUP BOATS ARE SO INCREDIBLY FAST?

Two years ago it was a big deal to hit 40 knots (46mph) in a 70ft Cup catamaran. Now it is normal for teams' test boats that are almost half that size to exceed those speeds.

Over the last five years the increase in performance for America's Cup boats is greater than at any point in the 164 year history of sailing's most prestigious event.

And we can thank the clever Kiwis at Emirates Team New Zealand for this dramatic turnaround in performance. Everyone knew that using hydrofoils to reduce the drag of the hulls by lifting the boats out of the water made them go twice as fast.

Yet there was no mention of foils in the America's Cup rules so the Kiwis quietly got on with developing their own systems. By the time the other teams cottoned on, ETNZ were well ahead of the game but a new die had been cast.

With foiling now established for the next America's Cup in 2017, the focus has been on making the foils more efficient. Creating more lift for less drag, while also achieving a foil that is stable and won't stall at speed and trip up the boat, has occupied much of the design teams' time.

Satisfying all these requirements has been a big technical challenge but it is here that motorsport has been embraced to provide the necessary hydraulic control technology.

"The systems required to control the foils are a new area for Cup teams," said Land Rover BAR's technical director Andy Claughton whose America's Cup experience stretches back over 30 years.

"To do this the crew has to manually pump the hydraulic fluid back and forth to effect the controls. The marine industry simply doesn't have this technology yet."

But motorsport does and it is here that Cup design teams have been applying motorsport technologies. The results have been dramatic.

'THE CONTROL SYSTEM REVOLUTION HAPPENED IN FORMULA ONE 20 YEARS AGO'

says former McLaren CEO, Martin Whitmarsh, now CEO, Land Rover BAR

The reliability of the systems has also surprised both designers and the sailors which has in turn meant that crews can push the boats much harder than they had previously expected.

The overall result is a steep learning curve and a rapid increase in performance.

Astronaut or athlete? Artemis' Chris Brittle kitted out to race

DRESSED TO THRILL

GONE ARE THE DAYS WHEN SAILORS TURNED UP TO RACE IN THE AMERICA'S CUP IN WHITE FLANNELS, A BLAZER AND CRAVAT.

The most technical pieces of sailing kit on a damp day were likely to be an oiled canvas jacket and sou-wester.

With the advent of the high speed foiling catamarans, it is now all about body armour, helmets, knives and personal breathing equipment. Sailors have started to look more like astronauts.

The changing safety requirements on the new America's Cup hydrofoil designs made the biggest impact with crews required to wear protection from the fast and powerful, predatory-looking, wingsail hydrofoils.

As well as helmets, and close-fitting body armour, each crew is required to carry a personal spare air tank and a safety knife, in case they become trapped under water during a capsize.

Paul Campbell-James – Land Rover BAR's wing trimmer – says the Spinlock buoyancy aid has been designed specifically.

"It has a built-in camel pack (for drinking water), a spine protector, a spare air breathing bottle and a knife. The breathing bottle and knife are positioned where they are easy to grab in an emergency.

"We do a lot of training in the water to ensure we are comfortable using these. The breather bottles provide about 30 seconds extra in the water if panicking, or four minutes when calm."

The Kask helmet used by the Land Rover BAR team have a built-in comms unit, earpiece and microphone.

Campbell-James added: "Each sailor has a different system depending on requirements. Ben Ainslie, for example, can be heard by all the crew at all times while I have a 'push to talk' feature so I can have a one to one conversation with the guy grinding the winch for me or I can speak to the whole crew."

In addition to the more conventional base layer kit such as Henry Lloyd wetsuits or drysuits in the winter (with rash vests or thermals underneath), the correct footwear is also important to ensure optimum grip.

Campbell-James concluded: "Most of us wear trail running shoes which are basically trainers with rubber spikes on the bottom, which give great grip on the trampoline."

UKSA
Sea. Change.

From weekend sailor to Professional Yachtmaster

Ready for a life at the helm? At UKSA you can train to be the next world's best sailor, learn how to crew the fastest sailing boats, and turn your passion for sailing into a full-time career.

We're a youth charity based on the Isle of Wight with a world-class training site at Cowes. We believe in the power of the water to transform people's lives for the better. But we also run professional courses that give our graduates everything they need to succeed at sea.

You can also join us for the day for more leisurely pursuits, or stay a bit longer and you could come away with a new qualification, and a new career. As a charity, we have funding available and our courses are suitable for everyone.

Book now and launch your career at sea.

Call **01983 203038**
Email **careers@uksa.org**
Visit **uksa.org**

#SeaChange
f UKSAsailing
▼ @UKSAsailing
◎ UKSAsailing

Professional   Development   Schools & Groups   Recreation   Charity

INTRODUCING THE NEW 50KTS RACE EDITION

TOTAL COMMITMENT™

SAIL RACING®
sailracing.com

FLYING MACHINES

THE AC45F IS THE RACING MACHINE THAT WILL SERVE AS DETONATOR TO THE DYNAMITE LOUIS VUITTON AMERICA'S CUP WORLD SERIES

t is a state-of-the-art catamaran (twin hulls) with a solid aeroplane wing-like sail and sexy go faster hydrofoils to provide lift, speed and an unbelievable wow factor.

This lightweight rocket ship, which can reach speeds of up to 50 knots, is a smaller version of the AC72, which was used in the 2013 Louis Vuitton Cup and the 34th America's Cup.

It was created as a relatively inexpensive boat to transport and sail so that teams could spend time on board to develop the skills needed to understand foil-style racing. It has also been invaluable in the development of the new AC48 which will be used for the 35th America's Cup.

To make racing as fair as possible the AC45F is a strict one-design, which means each boat is designed to the same set of rules and built from the same yard. The components on the boats such as the wingsail, crossbeams (which hold the two hulls together), the spine, and the bowsprit (the pointy spike at the front that supports the forward sail) are also manufacture controlled.

The development of hydrofoils in the last two years has created a totally new style of sailing that has seen even the world's best sailors – even Sir Ben Ainslie - having to learn new skills.

Gone are the days when it was possible to have the time to discuss tactics on the long run to the next mark. Now it is all about monitoring flap and foil angles, making decisions and completing manoeuvres in the blink of an eye and being fitter than an Ironman.

The AC45F is physically the hardest boat these sailors have ever sailed, said Land Rover BAR's wing trimmer Paul Campbell-James.

"It's a huge handful, but the rewards are big. Sailing at over 30kts in a fleet race is a truly awesome experience.

"My job is to trim the wing, which is a similar role to a mainsheet trimmer. Like every role on the boat, it is physically and mentally demanding.

"The loads are bigger than on a more conventional boat so being athletic and AC45-sailing fit is crucial.

"Ben at the helm is in charge of the lift of the boat with a hydraulic and battery-driven rake system controlled from a switch on a panel just in front of him. There's never a dull moment, that's for sure."

VITAL STATISTICS
TOUR AROUND THE AC45

1 Hydrofoil daggerboards lift the boat out of the water as the speed builds, reducing the drag of the hulls and helping the boats to achieve high speeds.

The daggerboards can be adjusted forwards and backwards at the top to alter the amount of lift that the horizontal part of the daggerboard provides. This adjustment is crucial. Too much angle and the boat wants to lift too readily, too little and the hulls won't lift off the surface.

2 The rudders have T-foils that raise the back end of the boat and ensure that the boat flies parallel to the water's surface

3 Instead of a conventional 'soft' mainsail, the AC45F has a wing like an aeroplane. They are 21.5m (70.5ft) tall and not only rotate so that they can be trimmed to the wind direction, but are built in two sections so they can be made to bend with the wind.

4 The AC45Fs have jibs for sailing upwind

5 Downwind the AC45Fs fly a gennnaker. The sail is furled up when hoisted and then unfurled when the helmsman calls 'deploy' to the crew.

6 Each boat is identical in the shape, design, structure and weight of the hulls, daggerboards, rudders, wing mast and sails. The jib and gennaker can be to a team's own design.

7 Each team consists of five crew – total maximum crew weight 437.5kg. The maximum weight per crew member of personal equipment is 6kg and each team can carry no more than 5kg of food and water. All teams are weighed before the start of each regatta.

8 The total minimum weight of the boat is 1320kg where the wingmast weighs 385kg. The light weight of the boat, the powerful sail plan and the ability to fly above the water's surface makes the AC45F a potent machine capable of speeds in excess of 35 knots (40mph).

DIMENSIONS OF THE AC45
Length: 13.45m (44.13ft)
Beam: 6.9m (22.6ft)
Weight: 1,320 kg (2910lbs)
Mast Height: 21.5m (70.5ft)
Sail Area: 133m2 (1430 ft2) upwind
Sail Area: 210m2 (2,259ft2) downwind

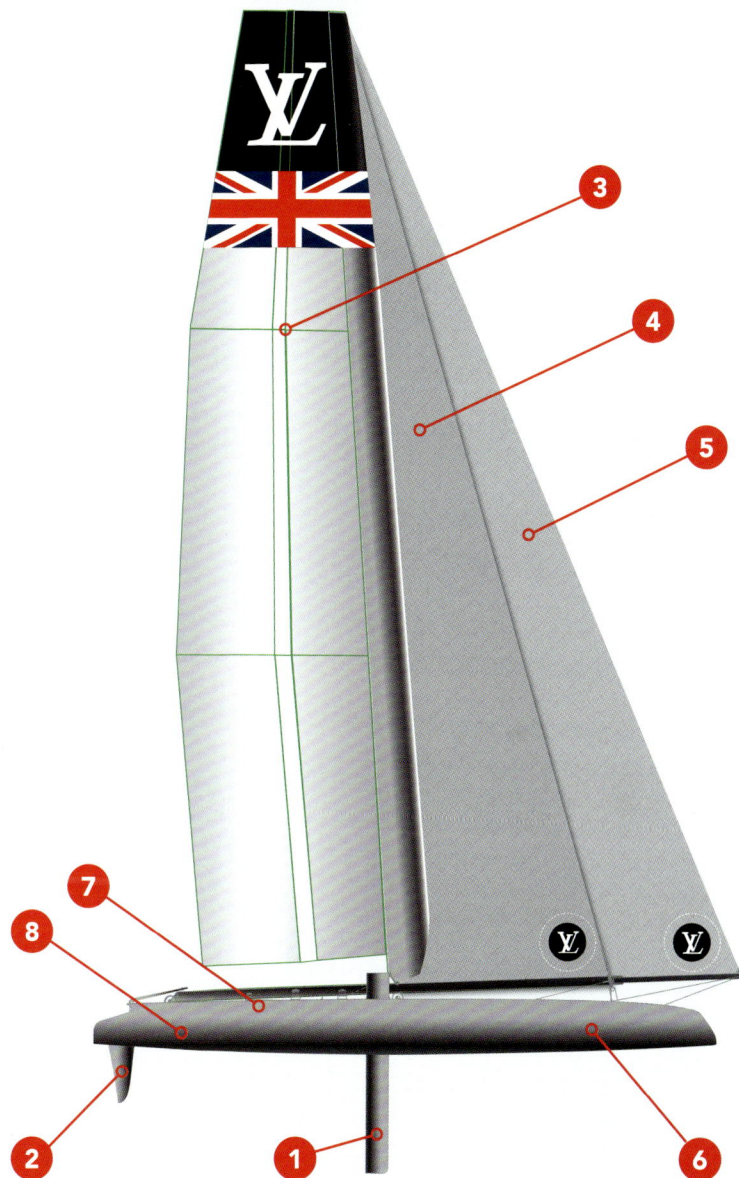

NEW ZEALAND

Emirates Team New Zealand is the most established sailing team in recent America's Cup history competing in all events since Fremantle 1987, except the 2010 Deed of Gift match. Two times winner of the America's Cup (1995 & 2000) and three times winner of the Louis Vuitton Cup (1995, 2007 & 2013) Emirates Team New Zealand has proven to be a leading innovator in sailing. It was the first team to introduce fibreglass to the America's Cup. Computational Fluid Dynamics (CFD), twisted flow wind tunnel modelling to mirror actual sailing conditions, the millennium rig mast in 2000 and real time sailing imagery to replicate sail shapes while racing are all New Zealand innovations. But most notably, Emirates Team New Zealand were the team to successfully develop and bring foiling into the mainstream of America's Cup and all of sailing. Emirates Team New Zealand remains the only commercially funded sailing team to survive since the multi-challenger event in Valencia in 2007.

Emirates TEAM NEW ZEALAND

ROYAL NEW ZEALAND YACHT SQUADRON

A THRIVING UNIVERSITY AT THE HEART OF A HISTORIC, VIBRANT AND FAST-CHANGING CITY.

We delight in creating, sharing and applying knowledge to make a difference to individuals and society.

Discover more
www.port.ac.uk

University of
Portsmouth

VISIT US

OPEN DAYS

Saturday 3 October 2015
Saturday 17 October 2015
Saturday 14 November 2015

GLENN **ASHBY**
SAILING TEAM DIRECTOR

DATE OF BIRTH: 01.09.77
NATIONALITY: AUS
BORN: Bendigo Australia
SAILING CLUB: Bendigo Yacht Club
STARTED SAILING: Aged 7
ROLE ON BOAT: Helmsman

AMERICA'S CUP:
2013: On Emirates Team New Zealand

AMERICA'S CUP WORLD SERIES:
2011, 2012, 2013: On Emirates Team New Zealand

Glenn Ashby is a multihull specialist with a distinguished record having 15 world championship titles plus sailing and coaching expertise in AC45s, AC72s, Extreme 40s, GC32s and A class catamaran. He was a member of the successful Oracle Racing team and head coach for the 2010 America's Cup challenge against Alinghi, in Valencia, Spain and was one of the first multihull experts to be hired by ETNZ. Ashby is a core member of the sailing team as Head of Sailing and is involved in the design process for the 35th America's Cup.

'AS A TEAM, IT'S AN EXCITING NEW CHAPTER FOR US TO GET ON THE WATER IN PORTSMOUTH AND SET SAIL ON OUR CONVERTED AC45F FOILING CATAMARAN. I FEEL WE WILL QUICKLY ADAPT AND SHOULD BE THROWING THE BOAT AROUND LIKE A DINGHY IN NO TIME'

GLENN ASHBY
SAILING TEAM DIRECTOR

PETER **BURLING**
HELMSMAN

DATE OF BIRTH: 01.01.91
NATIONALITY: NZL
BORN: Tauranga, NZL
SAILING CLUB: Tauranga Yacht and Powerboat Club
STARTED SAILING: Aged 8
ROLE ON BOAT: Helmsman

AMERICA'S CUP:
2013: Red Bull Youth America's Cup (Skipper)

Tauranga-born Peter Burling is one of the most exciting young sailing talents on the racing circuit. At 23 years old, Peter is already an Olympic medallist, a two-time Olympian, World Champion in the 49er in 2013 and 2014 (as well as World Championships silvers in 2011 and 2012), and a four-time winner of the New Zealand Young Sailor of the Year. At 17, he became the youngest ever sailor to represent New Zealand at the Olympic Games, competing in the 470 class as crew to Carl Evans. He was on the helm in the 49er skiff class when he and Blair Tuke won silver at the 2012 Olympic Games in London and the pair have won every event they competed in ever since. They were jointly named as 2013 New Zealand Sailors of the Year and joined ETNZ as a pair early in 2014. Burling's first appearance on the America's Cup circuit was in 2013 when he skippered the NZL Sailing Team to victory in the inaugural Youth America's Cup.

RAY DAVIES

DATE OF BIRTH: 22.11.71
NATIONALITY: NZL
BORN: Auckland
SAILING CLUB:
Murrays Bay Sailing Club
STARTED SAILING: Aged 6
ROLE ON BOAT: Tactician

AMERICA'S CUP:
2000: On America One
2007, 2013: On Emirates Team
New Zealand

AMERICA'S CUP WORLD SERIES:
2011, 2012, 2013: on Emirates
Team New Zealand

Helmsman and tactician Ray Davies has been has been a highly respected member of the Team NZ afterguard since the 2007 Americas Cup, helping the Kiwis win Louis Vuitton Trophies, Audi Med Cups and the Auld Mug itself. He has also raced around the world twice, and won the Volvo Ocean Race in 2001/2. Since the America's Cup became a multihull event, he has been polishing his racing and foiling skills in Extreme 40s, foiling Moths and A Class Catamarans at international level.

BLAIR TUKE

DATE OF BIRTH: 25.07.89
NATIONALITY: NZL
BORN: Kawakawa, NZL
SAILING CLUB: Kerikeri Cruising Club
STARTED SAILING: Aged 11
ROLE ON BOAT: Trimmer

AMERICA'S CUP:
2013: Red Bull Youth America's Cup on NZL Sailing Team with Emirates Team New Zealand

Blair is yet another young talent, before turning 20, he had two world championship titles to his name. Later he teamed up with Peter Burling to become double 49er World Champion and 2012 London Olympic silver medallist. He's no stranger to multihull racing too, having raced in the A Class. He was tactician for the winning NZL Sailing Team with ETNZ at the 2013 Red Bull Youth America's Cup in San Francisco. Blair Tuke joined the team early in 2014.

GUY ENDEAN

DATE OF BIRTH: 31.03.89
NATIONALITY: NZL
BORN: Auckland
SAILING CLUB: R.N.Z.Y.S
STARTED SAILING: Aged 10
ROLE ON BOAT: Grinder

AMERICA'S CUP:
2013: Red Bull Youth America's Cup on NZL Sailing Team with Emirates Team New Zealand.

Guy Endean started out sailing on dinghies in his home waters in New Zealand. As his professional career developed, he moved to bigger boats, competing in the Fastnet Race, Caribbean 600 and the Transatlantic Maxi Yacht Cup. In 2011/12 he worked on the shore crew with New Zealand's Volvo Ocean Race entry Camper with ETNZ.His debut on the America's Cup scene was in 2013, when he was a member the winning team led by helmsman Peter Burling in the Red Bull Youth America's Cup in San Francisco.

RIGHT: Sir Peter James Blake, KBE (1 October 1948 – 5 December 2001) led New Zealand to successive victories in the America's Cup. In honour of his services to yachting, Blake was appointed a Knight Commander of the Order of the British Empire in 1995

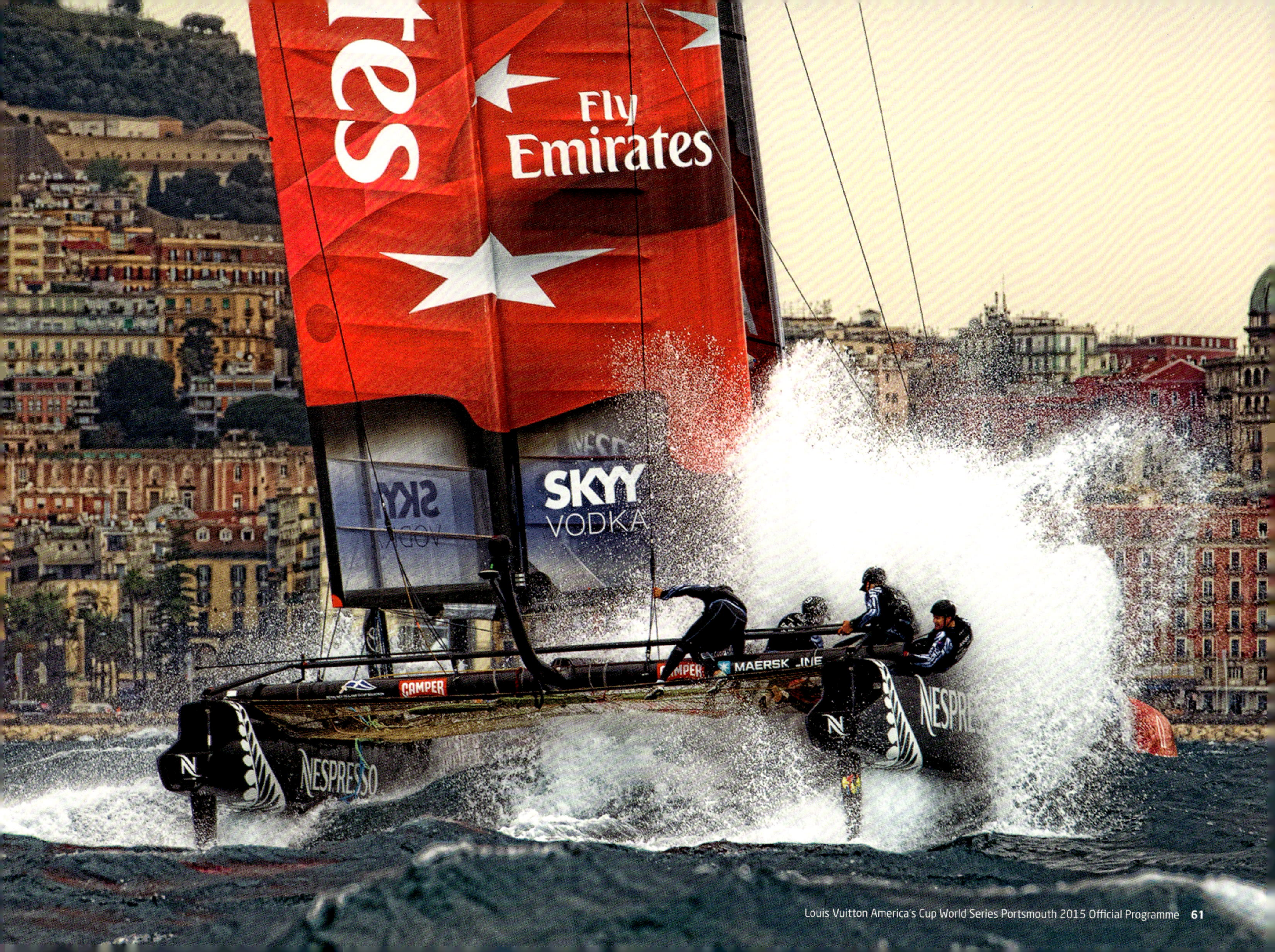
Fly
Emirates
SKYY
VODKA
CAMPER
MAERSK
NESPRESSO

SWEDEN

Artemis Racing's trophy collection across all racing classes is second to none with the sailors, designers and shore crew sharing countless America's Cup challenges and victories between them. The sailing team boasts an incredible 21 Olympic campaigns, seven Olympic gold medals and 27 World Championship titles. The team's principal, owner and founder, is Swedish entrepreneur Torbjörn Törnqvist, a passionate sailor and successful businessman who began one-design racing in 2005, taking several wins in the TP52 and RC44 class. Törnqvist's ambition is to win the America's Cup and bring the oldest trophy in sport to Sweden for the first time. Artemis Racing represents the Royal Swedish Yacht Club (KSSS), the fifth oldest yacht club in the world.

Artemis Racing

NATHAN OUTTERIDGE

DATE OF BIRTH: 28.01.86
NATIONALITY: AUS
BORN: Waratah, AUS
SAILING CLUB: Wangi Wangi
STARTED SAILING: Aged 5
ROLE ON BOAT: Skipper/Helmsman

AMERICA'S CUP:
2013: 34th America's Cup with Artemis Racing

AMERICA'S CUP WORLD SERIES:
2012: Team Korea
2013: Artemis Racing

Outteridge is one of Australia's most famous sailing names with one Olympic gold medal, four 49er World Championships and two International Moth Class World titles in his glittering collection. In 2009 he won the 49er World title with Artemis teammate Iain Jensen and the pair dominated the class for the next few years, winning Olympic gold at London 2012. Shortly after, he joined Artemis Racing as helmsman, aged just 27 and with is widely regarded as a specialist in foiling boats.

FREDRIK LÖÖF

DATE OF BIRTH: 13.12.69
NATIONALITY: SWE
BORN: Kristinehamn, SWE
SAILING CLUB: KSSS Royal Swedish Yacht Club
STARTED SAILING: Aged 3
ROLE ON BOAT: Tactician

An old friend and 'thorn in the side' of rival Iain Percy, Fredrik Lööf is one of the most successful Swedish sailors of all time. He has participated in six Olympic campaigns, beating Percy and Andrew Simpson to a gold medal in the Star class at London 2012. Fredrik won bronze in Beijing 2008 and bronze in the Finn class at Sydney 2000, where he was first pitted against Percy. Lööf's career highlights include three Finn World Championships, two Star World titles as well as a placed finish in the 2001-2002 Volvo Ocean Race with USA boat Pirates of the Caribbean. This is his first America's Cup campaign.

IAIN JENSEN

DATE OF BIRTH: 23.05.88
NATIONALITY: AUS
BORN: Belmont, AUS
SAILING CLUB: Wangi Wangi Sailing Club
STARTED SAILING: Aged 5
ROLE ON BOAT: Wing trimmer

AMERICA'S CUP:
2013: 34th America's Cup with Artemis Racing

Iain 'Goobs' Jensen was a schoolboy chum of Nathan Outteridge, the pair of them starting their sailing careers in Wangi Wangi on Australia's east coast. He represented Australia for the first time aged 16, winning the 420 Youth World Championships. In 2008, Jensen teamed up with Outteridge and almost immediately enjoyed success in the 49er class, winning the Worlds in 2009, 2011 and in 2012 and the gold medal at the London 2012 Olympic Games. Iain joined Artemis Racing shortly after as wing trimmer for the 34th America's Cup. At 26, this is his second America's Cup campaign.

CHRISTIAN KAMP

DATE OF BIRTH: 08.03.78
NATIONALITY: DEN
BORN: Kolding, Denmark
SAILING CLUB: Horsens Sejlklub
STARTED SAILING: Aged 9
ROLE ON BOAT: Trimmer

AMERICA'S CUP:
2005: 32nd America's Cup on Luna Rossa

Christian is one of Denmark's leading sailors though has spent much of his career racing for England and Italy! He was a member of the Luna Rossa Challenge for the 32nd America's Cup in 2007 then immediately after joined Britain's Team Origin where he raced with Iain Percy and Sir Ben Ainslie in the Louis Vuitton Pacific Series, the Audi MedCup TP52 and the World Match Racing Tour, winning the World title in 2010. He has competed on the RC44 and Extreme Sailing Series circuits and career highlights include three world championships, one European and three national titles.

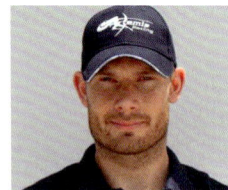

CHRIS BRITTLE

DATE OF BIRTH: 08.10.81
NATIONALITY: GBR
BORN: Rearsby, Leicestershire
SAILING CLUB: Roundhill Sailing Club
STARTED SAILING: Aged 4
ROLE ON BOAT: Grinder

AMERICA'S CUP:
2007: +39 Challenge
2013: on Artemis Racing

AMERICA'S CUP WORLD SERIES:
2011: Team Korea
2012: Artemis Racing

Brittle is regarded as a tour de force in sailing due to his powerhouse physique, which makes him the 'ultimate' grinder. Until 2007, he was part of the British Olympic squad campaigning a Finn but has raced in a number of classes and international circuits. These include the 32nd America's Cup where he raced on +39 Challenge (with Iain Percy) as a grinder, the Volvo Ocean Race and the Audi MedCup. From 1999 to 2005, Brittle was Ben Ainslie's training partner through the 2004 Olympics and coached Iain Percy and Andrew Simpson in Beijing 2008 where they won gold. This is his second campaign with the team.

PAUL GOODISON

DATE OF BIRTH: 29.11.77
NATIONALITY: GBR
BORN: Sheffield, UK
SAILING CLUB: Ulley Sailing Club, Rotherham
STARTED SAILING: Aged 5
ROLE ON BOAT: Reserve Helmsman

Paul brings a wealth of Olympic experience to Artemis Racing, having competed at the 2004 Athens, 2008 Beijing, where he won a gold medal and 2012 London Games. He is also a former Laser World Champion claiming the 2009 title in Halifax, Canada. Since the London Olympics, Paul has won the Melges 32 World Championships in 2012 and the Melges 20 World Championships in 2014, while also sailing in the 2014 Extreme Sailing Series with Land Rover BAR. More recently, Paul has been developing his foiling skill set, training and competing in the Moth, claiming a respectable 12th place in his first ever Moth Worlds in 2014.

IAIN **PERCY**

DATE OF BIRTH: 21.03.76
NATIONALITY: GBR
BORN: Southampton
SAILING CLUB: Stokes Bay SC / Hayling Island SC
STARTED SAILING: Aged 6
ROLE ON BOAT: Team Manager

AMERICA'S CUP:
2007: 32nd America's Cup with +39 Challenge
2013: 34th America's Cup with Artemis Racing

AMERICA'S CUP WORLD SERIES:
2011/2012/2013 with Artemis Racing

Iain Percy is one of the world's most successful sailors with two Olympic gold medals (Finn, Sydney 2000 and Star, Beijing 2008) and a silver (Star, London 2012) plus two World Championship titles. He began his career sailing at Weston Sailing Club in Southampton, UK in an Optimist dinghy. He completed a degree in Economics and just two years later was representing Great Britain at the 2000 Sydney Olympics. In 2005, he joined +39 Challenge as helmsman in his first America's Cup campaign before teaming up with lifelong friend Andrew 'Bart' Simpson for more Olympic success at Beijing 2008 and London 2012. He retired from Olympic sailing in 2012 when he became skipper of the 34th America's Cup Challenger of Record Artemis Racing in San Francisco. In May 2013, Bart, who had also joined Artemis Racing, was tragically killed in a training accident which left the team and the entire sailing community shocked and bereft. In October 2013 Percy was appointed Team Manager and is now responsible for leading the team's challenge for the 35th America's Cup.

'I AM PROUD TO BE BRITISH, BUT IN PORTSMOUTH, I'LL BE DOING EVERYTHING I CAN TO MAKE SURE THE SWEDISH (ARTEMIS RACING) ARE FIRST ACROSS THE FINISH LINE.'

USA

ORACLE TEAM USA was founded in 2000 by American businessman Larry Ellison to enter the 2003 America's Cup in Auckland. They reached the finals of the Louis Vuitton Cup losing 5-1 to Alinghi but quickly bounced back to become Challenger of Record in 2007 in Valencia where they reached the semi-finals of the Louis Vuitton Cup. For 2010, Ellison hired the America's Cup's most successful sailor in history Russell Coutts and finally achieved Oracle's first win. The 33rd America's Cup was a Deed of Gift match in Valencia but Ellison's giant 90' trimaran easily outclassed the Swiss holder Alinghi. Three years later in San Francisco, the Defender was facing a crushing defeat in the finals against Emirates Team New Zealand when at 8-1 down, they staged an historic comeback to win 9-8. The ORACLE TEAM USA team represents San Francisco's Golden Gate Yacht Club.

ORACLE®
TEAM USA

GOLDEN GATE
YACHT CLUB

BREMONT

(4)

ORACLE TEAM USA

DRIVE RESPONSIBLY.

BMW i8, the world's most progressive sports car, is now World Green Car of the Year 2015. Combining sports car performance with ultra-low emissions, this hybrid re-defines the meaning of driving pleasure.

becomeelectric.co.uk/i8

BMW i

BMW
The Ultimate
Driving Machi

WORLD GREEN CAR
2015 WORLD CAR AWARDS

VCC 115

Official fuel economy figures for the BMW i8: Weighted combined cycle: mpg 134.5 (2.1 l/100 km), CO₂ emissions 49 g/km, power output (engine) 170/231 kW/hp, power output (electric motor) 96/131 kW/hp, total average energy consumption per 62 miles/100 km (weighted combined cycle) 11.9 kWh, customer-orientated total range up to 373 miles. Maximum electric range value 23 miles, common average electric range value (e-Drive only) up to 23 miles. Figures may vary depending on different factors, including but not limited to individual driving style, climatic conditions, route characteristics and preconditioning. The BMW i8 is a plug in hybrid electric vehicle that requires mains electricity for charging.

'IT'S BEEN A WHILE SINCE OUR LAST RACE SO WE'RE LOOKING FORWARD TO LINING UP AND SEEING HOW WE MEASURE UP. WE'LL HAVE A TARGET ON OUR BACK AS DEFENDING CHAMPIONS BUT WE HAVE A GREAT TEAM WHO ARE HUNGRIER THAN EVER'

JAMES SPITHILL

DATE OF BIRTH: 28.06.79
NATIONALITY: AUS
BORN: Sydney, Australia
SAILING CLUB: Avalon Sailing Club
STARTED SAILING: Aged 4
ROLE ON BOAT: Skipper

AMERICA'S CUP:
2000: with Young Australia
2003: with One World
2007: with Prada Luna Rossa
2010: with BMW Oracle (giant trimaran)
2013: with Oracle Team USA

In helming ORACLE TEAM USA to victory in 2010, James Spithill became the youngest skipper to ever win the America's Cup. Yet his story with the Trophy dates back to when he was growing up on his native Scotland Island in Pittwater, just north of Sydney when he became gripped by Australia's success in the sport during the 80s. At the age of just 9, he told his family his goal was to become an America's Cup sailor and he was as good as his word. By 19, he had become the youngest skipper in America's Cup history racing with Young Australia and at 30, he won his first Cup. He would add a second just three years later. Known for his aggressive start tactics, his nickname was "James Pitbull" when he raced with Luna Rossa in the 2007 Cup. Despite his singular focus on the America's Cup, he has grown into one of the world's best all round sailors with multiple world championships under his belt.

ORACLE
TEAM USA

TOM SLINGSBY

DATE OF BIRTH: 05.09.84
NATIONALITY: AUS
BORN: Wahroonga, Australia
SAILING CLUB: Gosford YC
STARTED SAILING: Aged 6
ROLE ON BOAT: Tactician

AMERICA'S CUP:
2013: with Oracle Team USA

One of the most naturally gifted sailors in the world with eight world titles and one Olympic gold medal from London 2012 (Laser) to his name, Tom Slingsby made his debut in the America's Cup in 2013 with the role of strategist on board winning boat Oracle Team USA. Previously, his career had mostly revolved around dinghies but he shifted easily to the international match-racing circuit, big boat and high performance catamaran (Extreme 40, GC32, Moth) campaigns. In 2012 he was nominated Australian Athlete of the Year.

KYLE LANGFORD

DATE OF BIRTH: 30.07.89
NATIONALITY: AUS
BORN: Sydney
SAILING CLUB: Lake Macquarie YC
STARTED SAILING: Aged 6
ROLE ON BOAT: Trimmer

AMERICA'S CUP:
2013: with Oracle Team USA

Kyle Langford may be young but already boasts an America's Cup win. At 24 he was the youngest sailor on Oracle Team USA during their successful defence in 2013. He learned to sail on Lake Maquarie, north of Sydney and went on to race in different classes including the 49er, Laser and Tornado, appearing on the match-racing, RC44 and Extreme Sailing Series circuits. In 2006 was nominated Australia's Youth Sailor of the Year.

KINLEY FOWLER

DATE OF BIRTH: 28.11.87
NATIONALITY: AUS
BORN: Wellington NZL
SAILING CLUB: Royal Perth Yacht Club
STARTED SAILING: Aged 9
ROLE ON BOAT: Trimmer

AMERICA'S CUP:
2013: with Oracle Team USA

AMERICA'S CUP WORLD SERIES:
ACWS 2012 with Team Oracle USA

Kinley Fowler was born in New Zealand, raised in Australia and started sailing late but once he got going there was no stopping him. He took part in match-racing events during high school before moving to Europe to start his professional sailing career. After several years and successes on the match-racing circuit, the America's Cup opportunity came knocking when he took a volunteer shore crew job with Oracle Team USA in the 2012 ACWS. Determined and hardworking, Kinley succeeded in getting a spot in OTUSA's sailing team and won the America's Cup in 2013.

LOUIS SINCLAIR

DATE OF BIRTH: 30.10.91
NATIONALITY: NZL but lives in Antigua
BORN: Auckland
SAILING CLUB: Antigua YC
STARTED SAILING: Aged 6
ROLE ON BOAT: Bowman

Born in New Zealand, Louis Sinclair grew up and started sailing in Antigua completing his first races in the Optimist class. While racing in the Caribbean at the age of 16, he began working on a classic 80' yacht owned by the father of Antiguan sailor Shannon Falcone who was later to become his Oracle Team USA teammate. Louis is a passionate offshore sailor having being bowman on ICAP Leopard and the 100-footer Comanche and was one of the under 30 crew members of Abu Dhabi, which recently won the 2014-2015 Volvo Ocean Race.

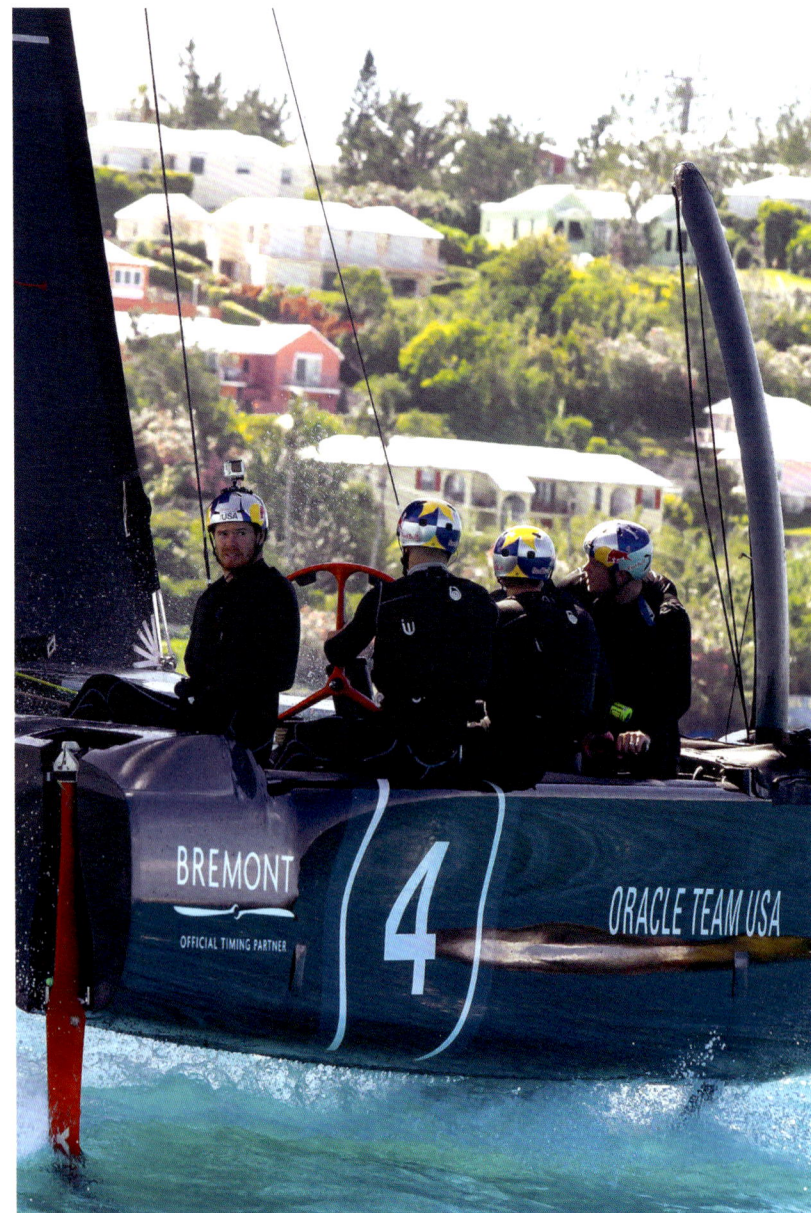

Haslar Marina...

the perfect location

Situated at the very heart of Portsmouth Harbour, with fast connections to London, the Solent and beyond.

Enjoy the views over this bustling harbour from the green Lightship's sun decks.

Quality facilities, the warmest welcome and two great restaurants on-site.

HASLAR MARINA

35R

Tel: 023 9260 1201   www.haslarmarina.co.uk

DEAN & REDDYHOFF MARINAS   PORTLAND   WEYMOUTH   HASLAR   EAST COWES

Bermuda's National Drink Has Quite A Bit In Common With Her National Party Day.

*I*magine a regatta of 14-foot boats, each with 1,000 squarefeet of sail and six crewmen. It gets better: These crewmen function as moveable—and often *disposable*—ballast, as the skipper can order (or shove) as many overboard as he deems fit to gain speed!

This outrageous competition has been a key ingredient of the annual Bermuda Day festivities for over 150 years. As has Gosling's Black Seal Rum.

In fact, Bermuda's Official National Drink is our Dark 'n Stormy.® A bracing, refreshing mix of two ounces of Black Seal added to a highball glass with ice cubes and almost filled with ginger beer (ideally Gosling's own). Lime optional, enjoyment mandatory. Simple, but simply delicious. And, a little spicy.

Could be Bermuda's not quite as tame as you thought it was.

Gosling's. For Seven Stubborn Generations.

VICTORY AT ANY COST

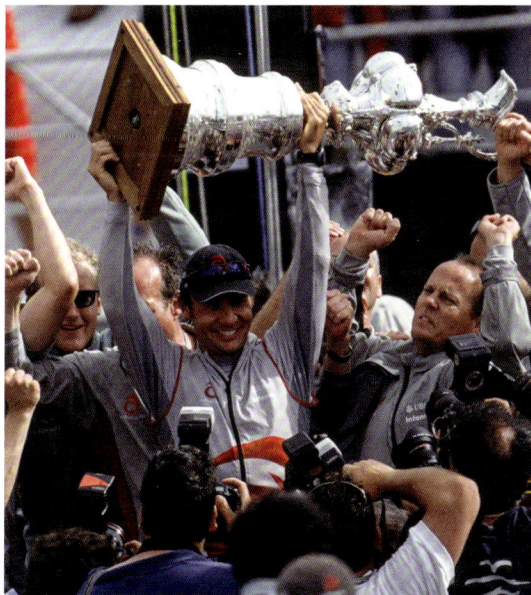

Funding an America's Cup campaign has been eye-wateringly expensive from the outset since super-fast boats have either meant big lavish affairs or small highly engineered guided missiles.

When Nat Herreshoff, the 'Wizard of Bristol' created the biggest ever Cup yacht Reliance in 1903, it was 144 ft long with 16,160 sq.ft sails on masts that reached 189ft into the sky.

Built for a syndicate of robber barons that included J P Morgan, Wm Rockefeller and Cornelius Vanderbilt, she cost a whopping £115,000 or £80 million in today's money.

Her crew of 64 were each paid around 65p a day representing a monthly crew bill of £2500 (six days a week only) or £35 per man per month which equates to a £4000 a month pay packet in 2015.

Compare that with the current America's Cup salary. These days, a modest grinder might command £16,000 per month with extra housing allowance and other

Costs have risen dramatically in the America's Cup. In 2013, teams spent hundreds of millions of pounds

expenses. Skippers and tacticians might bank up to twice or three times that figure.

Much of this investment came from deep private pockets so not surprisingly, estimates of costs, budgets, funds and expenses are guesswork.

While the world economic situation improved, the costs of challenging rose too. In the 1990s, Bill Koch's America3 team cost £46 million, with a third spent on research and design and crew costs amounting to more than £6 million. Research costs escalated with the size of design teams. One top team had 40 engineers as well as hydro and aerodynamicists at an average monthly salary of around £4,500. For three years, the bill might amount to well over £2 million for the team.

So it is little wonder that today's teams have started to look for ways to reduce costs down from campaign budgets that could otherwise approach £100 million. The complexity of the boat construction demands the best available manpower for any team to have a serious chance of success. But the new, smaller, America's Cup Class will help ease the impact on the overall budget.

TOP LEFT: Old J Class boats required more than 30 crew

TOP RIGHT: Design costs have spiralled with new technology

BOTTOM LEFT: Swiss entrepreneur Ernesto Bertorelli invested millions into winning the America's Cup

Q8

Sir Keith Mills

Sir Keith Mills is Britain's leading sports entrepreneur. He led the team that won London's Olympic bid in 2005, raised £2.4 billion in Olympic revenues and was Deputy chairman of LOCOG, the organising committee that made it the most successful Olympic Games in history.

He then worked alongside HRH Prince Harry to create last year's Invictus Games before turning his attention to the one sporting trophy Britain has never managed to win. The America's Cup.

OPPOSITE: Sir Keith Mills on receiving the Lifetime Achievement Award for his support and contribution to sport at the Sport Industry Group UK Awards 2015. (Image courtesy of Getty Images)

A

The America's Cup seems to be the most addictive sporting trophy. What's the big deal and why do successful businessmen become so obsessed with winning it?

Successful businessmen get a big kick from being part of a sports team and helping them succeed because that's what they do in their business lives. Most of them are unbelievably competitive and get a real thrill out of winning. I personally find winning intoxicating. The moment in Singapore when they announced that London had won the Olympic Games was fantastically exciting, and winning the America's Cup will be equally exciting. More exciting perhaps because Britain has never won it before. Being part of a team that makes that happen is very special.

Sir Charles Dunstone and yourself are the main investors behind Land Rover BAR. How much will you have spent by the end of the next Cup in 2017?

The whole campaign, including our new base, will have cost more than £100 million and although our shareholders have invested a considerable amount, a large percentage will come from commercial revenues. This is a sporting challenge but it is also a business challenge, a high risk one. Our objective is firstly to win the America's Cup because if we do that, our yacht club, The Royal Yacht Squadron, becomes trustee of the Cup and the rules allow us to take control so that we can transform it into a more sustainable sport. We are investing a lot of money now in the expectation that we and our corporate partners will get a return. The America's Cup in Valencia in 2007 produced a significant return for the city, for the corporate partners and for the shareholders and other stakeholders.

How important is Sir Ben Ainslie to the success of this campaign?

We would or could not have done it with anyone else. To make something like this work you need an extraordinary individual and Ben is an extraordinary sportsman. Everyone is drawn to the team because of Ben. Sailors, designers, sponsors, spectators, media. The time is right now to make our bid. The stars are aligned. Watching Ben get on the US boat in San Francisco in 2013 and watching that magnificent come back was a sort of Eureka moment. Sir Charles Dunstone and I realised that Ben needed an opportunity to do it. We were on the phone that week discussing how we could get behind Ben to give him that opportunity.

Can you talk us through how you organise an America's Cup campaign from scratch?

You start by getting together an exceptionally talented group of people and that is exactly what Ben has done. You then need to build a business plan that details all of the costs and potential revenues and produce a budget and an operating plan that gives you the best chance of winning. An America's Cup team is not dissimilar to a Formula One team where the margins between success and failure are tiny. The design and build of the race boats, like F1, is hugely technical these days. Massive amounts of computing power and the world's best engineers and designers. The skills and fitness of the sailing team are critical so the training programmes are relentless and tough. Finally winning any major sporting trophy is a massive team effort and needs strong leadership. In Ben Ainslie we have an extraordinary Team Principal and the world's greatest sailor and he is now supported by Martin Whitmarsh who has joined BAR from McClaren where he was CEO.

Is this just about winning a sporting trophy or will there be other benefits?

Winning the America's Cup will open up many other opportunities. Firstly, we have built an iconic new base for BAR in Portsmouth. We want to use the base to accelerate the regeneration of Portsmouth by attracting new developments and other marine based businesses, as Formula 1 has done. Secondly, we have established a new charity, the 1851 Trust, which I chair. With The Duchess of Cambridge and Ben Ainslie as our Patrons, we aim to use the America's Cup to support a number of programmes designed to inspire and engage young people. We will focus on youth sailing, STEM education, the marine environment and marine training and apprenticeships. The Olympics led to the regeneration of East London and inspired millions of young people and this is what we are hoping to achieve with the Cup. Over the next few years we would hope to have an America's Cup racing team which is sustainable and the best in the world. We will have started to develop other businesses off the back of the team like applied technology and marine businesses and a foundation which is putting a lot of money into a whole range of projects to encourage the next generation.

Why have an America's Cup World Series event in Portsmouth?

The impact of the Cup in San Francisco in 2013 surprised us all including me and now we have a format with a fantastic potential to capture television audiences and live spectators which will be attractive to millions. We will have hundreds and thousands of spectators in Portsmouth to watch the racing, which is unheard of in the sport of sailing. We would love the British public to get behind Ben and build an Olympic type fever around the campaign so we are working really hard with our TV and media partners, as well as with our corporate partners like Land Rover to make this happen.

What happens if you don't win?

We don't contemplate that. We have a great team and a ruthless determination to succeed. In our Olympic bid nobody gave us much chance of winning, but with the right team everything is possible. We will make history and bring the Cup home to Britain for the first time in over 160 years.

Facts & Figures

4 Nations have only ever won the America's Cup:

🇺🇸 **USA**

🇳🇿 **New Zealand**

🇦🇺 **Australia**

🇨🇭 **Switzerland**

USA successfully defended the America's Cup for 132 years facing 25 challenges before they lost it to Australia in 1983.

It was the longest winning streak in sporting history

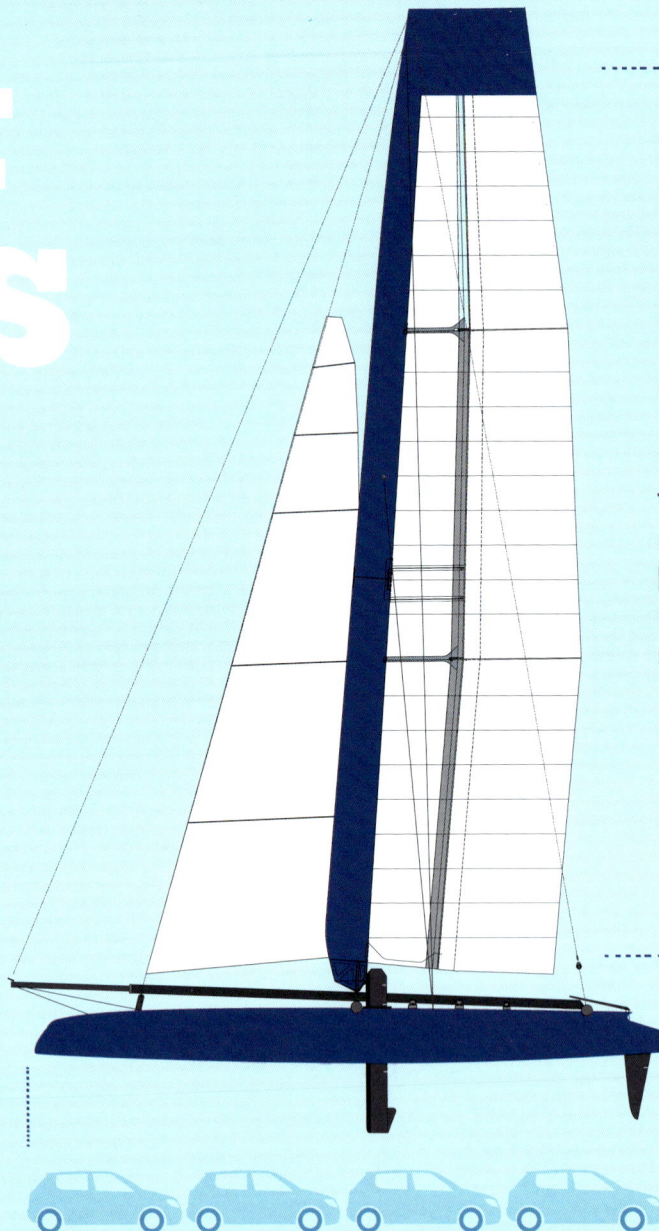

70ft

The AC45F wing mast is **70 feet high**. The same height as a seven storey building

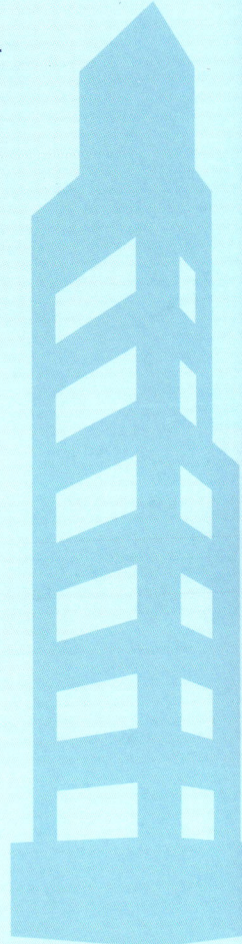

45ft

The AC45F is 45 feet in length equivalent to **4 family cars.**

42

42mph - maximum speed recorded by AC45F.

34 America's Cups...

have been staged in just SEVEN venues: **New York** (USA), **Newport, Rhode Island** (USA), **Fremantle** (Australia), **San Diego** (USA), **Auckland** (New Zealand), **Valencia** (Spain) and **San Francisco** (USA)

400 metres of rope is pulled per race

The **America's Cup World Series** in Plymouth in September 2011 cost the City Council **£225,000** but generated more than **£9 million** in revenue for the local economy.

The **34th America's Cup** in San Francisco was broadcast to **190** countries with over **100 million** minutes watched in September 2013. App downloads were over **430,000**. YouTube views over **27.3 million**

170 bmp...

A sailor's heart rate can exceed during racing...

The **America's Cup Park** and **America's Cup Village** in San Francisco recorded over **1 million visitors**. A record number of Kiwis tuned in to watch ETNZ lose the 2013 final in San Francisco, peaking at 1.2 million viewers, which was higher than for Black Magic's historic win in 1995.

If Sir Ben Ainslie wasn't a sailor he would want to be an F1 racing driver

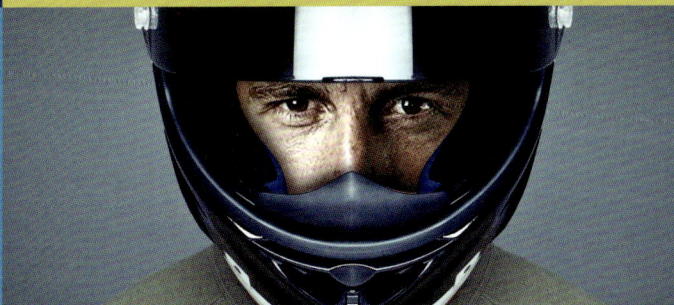

The **beefiest sailors** on the AC45 are the grinders who have to put out enough torque to control the 3,000-pound wing sail.

Oracle Team USA skipper Jimmy Spithill was the youngest sailor ever to helm an America's Cup boat (19) and the youngest skipper to win the Americas Cup (30).

Approximately **9.25 million tourists** visited Portsmouth last year and they spent **£444m**. Almost 12% of everyone with a job in Portsmouth works in tourism.

The **Oracle Team USA** crew all incorporate boxing into their training regime to improve their hand and eye coordination.

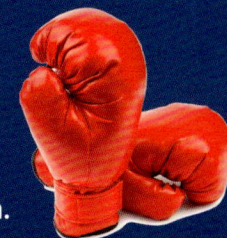

1851 TRUST

THE LAUNCH OF THE 1851 TRUST AT LAND ROVER BAR HEADQUARTERS IN PORTSMOUTH IN OCTOBER 2014 WAS JUST THE SPARK NEEDED TO REIGNITE PUBLIC INTEREST IN THE AMERICA'S CUP AND SHOWCASE WHAT THE BRITISH AIM TO ACHIEVE

Sir Ben Ainslie CBE and his hand-picked team at Land Rover BAR immediately captured public interest at the event with the announcement that Her Royal Highness the Duchess of Cambridge would support the 1851 Trust as Royal Patron.

Although the team's quest to win the America's Cup for Britain for the first time ever is a priority, the aim in setting up the 1851 Trust – a new charitable division of Land Rover BAR – is to create a legacy that will help future generations engage in sailing and learn about exciting technologies in the marine sector.

In similar style to Formula 1 racing, the America's Cup leads the way in technology with the yachts and equipment in a constant state of development. America's Cup racing is at the hub of marine technology and, through the 1851 Trust, Sir Ben and his team are passionate to share their knowledge and inspire a new generation.

With a philosophy that embraces technology and innovation, it is befitting that the Trust was named in recognition of the 1851 Great Exhibition. Not only was 1851 a pivotal point in the progress of industry, it was also an evolutionary period in shipbuilding and design.

The idea of the 1851 Trust is for young people under the age of 25, from diverse backgrounds, to benefit from

its work. The aim is to educate and help build the skills required for the racing sailors and innovators of the future.

Alasdair Akass – CEO of the 1851 Trust – says they hoped to make a real difference to young people both on and off the water, and make a concerted effort to challenge, and counter the perceived and real barriers that prevent youngsters taking to the water.

"We want to harness the power of the America's Cup to inspire not just the next crew, but also to showcase the amazing stake that engineers, designers and a plethora of other talented individuals have in the development of the British team," he said.

"We also want to create a social conscience about how protecting the marine environment now will have a significant effect in the future."

To be effective, the Trust aims to make vocational entry into maritime industry more appealing. Their idea is to work closely with maritime organisations to offer viable apprenticeships and pathways into the industry sector.

Among a powerful line-up of Trustees that includes Sir Keith Mills GBE (chairman), Claire Locke (founder of Italian fashion house Artigiano) and Lady Georgie Ainslie, is Rod Carr CBE, the former CEO of the Royal Yachting Association.

"The 1851 Trust is about the future and embracing golden opportunities," he said.

"It will be the total opposite to a museum. The whole idea is to create an environment that looks to the future and not the past. The exciting technology on show will hopefully inspire youngsters to not only get involved with sailing through schools, sailing clubs and other organisations, but to seek career opportunities within the marine industry."

An overwhelming show of support by local communities of a recent themed art project in Portsmouth couldn't have been a better way to kick-start The 1851 Trust.

Designed to celebrate the maritime heritage of the Solent, the project involved a total of 72 students from six schools

"WE ALSO WANT TO CREATE A SOCIAL CONSCIENCE ABOUT HOW PROTECTING THE MARINE ENVIRONMENT NOW WILL HAVE A SIGNIFICANT EFFECT IN THE FUTURE"

across Portsmouth and Ryde. With guidance from local street artists James Waterfield and Dharma 77, the group teamed up to a paint a mural on the hoardings of the construction site at the new Land Rover BAR headquarters.

Although the Trust Visitor Centre, located at those headquarters at Camber Quay, won't be officially open to the public until the end of the year, exciting developments to create an interactive showcase for the sport are well underway.

Special features will include a unique virtual sailing experience that gives those who have never been in a sailboat a realistic idea of what it's like to race at the top of the sport, with tips and advice from Land Rover BAR team members.

Other innovative features on display at the Centre include a 3D printer that produces custom parts for the race boats and the sailing team's funky Power Grinder fitness trainer.

Information on how clubs and organisations can benefit from the work of the Trust, plus details on how to make a donation, visit 1851trust.org.uk.

"SUMMER AFTERNOON;
TO ME THOSE HAVE ALWAYS BEEN THE TWO MOST
BEAUTIFUL WORDS IN THE ENGLISH LANGUAGE"
HENRY JAMES

DESTINATION
BERTHON | SUMMER
VALETING | MAINTENANCE
& REPAIRS | BERTHON
SERVICE

DID YOU KNOW THAT BERTHON BOAT COMPANY HAS COMPLETED 350 RIB REFITS IN THE LAST FIVE YEARS?

BERTHON

SYNONYMOUS WITH YACHTING SINCE 1877

The Shipyard, Bath Road, Lymington, Hampshire SO41 3YL

Find out what Berthon can do for you this Season
www.berthon.co.uk

Follow us on Twitter and Like us on Facebook @BerthonGroup

Phone 44 (0) 1590 673312   Email enquiries@berthon.co.uk

1851 TRUST
VISITOR CENTRE

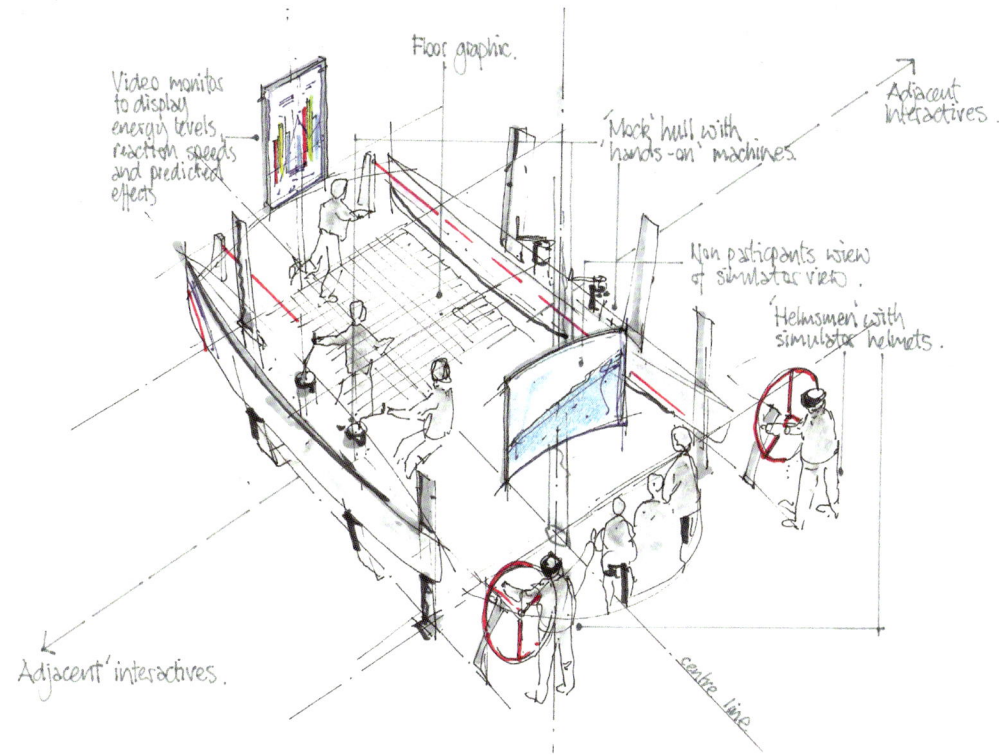

THE OPPORTUNITY TO CAMPAIGN FOR AMERICA'S CUP OPENS UP A WEALTH OF ADDITIONAL AVENUES, INCLUDING A CHANCE TO INSPIRE FUTURE GENERATIONS TO PRESERVE AND NURTURE OUR MARINE ENVIRONMENT

Plans for a dynamic new visitor centre in the Portsmouth headquarters of Ben Ainslie Racing will aim to do just that.

It will represent a major cornerstone of the 1851 Trust's mission to use sailing as a platform for education and training, presenting the sport in a way that stimulates a wider interest in sustainability and innovation and promotes the Trust's STEM agenda – focussing on Science, Technology, Engineering and Mathematics in schools and universities.

The Visitor Centre will be one of a kind in the UK. Dynamic, inspirational and following the narrative

"How to Win the America's Cup", where visitors get to sample a range of different experiences.

These include meeting members of the Land Rover BAR Racing team whose skill set covers the full spectrum of talents and careers from all types of engineering through to design, management, logistics and operations.

The Land Rover BAR racing team employs the best and most passionate specialists in sports science, communications, marketing and of course sailing where only world-class qualifies.

Visitors will also have a lesson in history by journeying through 164 years of compelling dramas that have

sustained the America's Cup and made it the most coveted trophy in sailing.

They will get an opportunity to understand the technology and innovation behind the spectacular foiling AC45Fs and even get to sail them, which will leave them in no doubt as to the physical challenge involved in being an America's Cup sailor and the additional skills required to get a boat round a course.

The themes of sustainability and the health of the oceans will cut across the experience and help underpin one of the 1851 Trust's core objectives to help create future stewards of the marine environment. The Visitor Centre is planned to open before the end of the year.

How to follow the Louis Vuitton America's Cup World Series Racing...

All boats are carrying tracking devices so you can follow their progress on the race course at www.americascup.com. There are many other ways to keep up to date

Television

BT Sport

BT Sport is the UK Live Host Broadcaster for the 2015 - 2017 America's Cup. During the 2015 Portsmouth event they will show all racing action live on BT Sport and will do the same for all other Louis Vuitton America's Cup World Series events.

BBC

BBC is the UK Highlights Host Broadcaster for the 2015 - 2017 America's Cup. During the 2015 Portsmouth event they will show a half hour evening highlights show on the Saturday and Sunday evening as well as an event hour long highlights show on the Monday evening after the event.

Radio

A live radio broadcast available at Portsmouth **Live Radio on 93.7 fm** covering the area from Southampton to Chichester. Brought to you by the same expert sailing commentators who have been presenting Cowes Radio for the past 30 years.

Steve Ancsell, Matt Sheahan and former Portsmouth Mayor and local radio favourite Cheryl Buggy will start their live broadcasts each day 30 minutes before racing until 30 minutes after with previews, reviews and interviews throughout the build up plus commentary from out on the race track. Radio is also available online at **www.ybw.co.uk, www.dailysail.co.uk** and **www.sailradio.co.uk** plus an audio stream app for smartphones and tablets.

Mobile

Americas Cup APP:

The America's Cup App is one of the best ways to follow your favourite America's Cup sailors on the go with all the latest news and photos, as well as up to the minute results from the water. Subscribe to AC+ to unlock special rich content features. The AC App is available for iOS and Android devices.

Live BLOG:

Don't miss out on all the results, reaction, updates and gossip behind the scenes with our live blog on **www.acwsportsmouth.com**

Live RESULTS:

Results will be updated at the end of each race at **www.americascup.com** with points and ranking updated in real time.

Facebook:

Our Facebook page Louis Vuitton America's Cup World Series Portsmouth is the best place to cast your eye across all the action for news and updates on racing and entertainments across all four days. **www.facebook.com/acwsportsmouth**

Twitter:

Instant news and pictures at **@acwspmth**

Website:

www.acwsportsmouth.com
www.americascup.com

THE FIRST BRITISH OFFICIAL TIMING PARTNER
TO THE AMERICA'S CUP SINCE 1851.

Visit our Boutique in the America's Cup Fanzone to discover the new
Bremont America's Cup Special Edition Collection.

AMERICA'S CUP | BREMONT OFFICIAL TIMING PARTNER | ORACLE TEAM USA

BREMONT.COM/AMERICASCUP

Presenters in Fanzone and Waterfront Arenas

Helen Bulkeley

Has worked in television production for over 10 years and has produced programmes and reported at events around the world including the 34th America's Cup, the Olympics and the Volvo Ocean Race.

Guy Swindells

Sports broadcaster and events host who has worked for the BBC, Sky, ITV, IRN and TalkSport covering the Olympic Games, Round the Island Race, Ryder Cup, Wimbledon, Rugby World Cups, Premier League football and Test cricket.

Andy Green

Former America's Cup sailor who competed in 2000 and 2003 and expert sailing TV commentator for live world feed on Americascup TV, live TV for Monsoon Cup and kept Olympic audiences entertained throughout sailing competition in Weymouth at London 2012 Olympics.

Abi Griffiths

Host of BT Sport's MotoGP and its flagship motorsport programme Motorsport Tonight but turned her hand to beach volleyball, hockey, wheelchair basketball and Paralympic Goalball at London 2012 and also presents on boxing.

Live TV Commentators

Ken Read

American yachtsman Ken Read was relatively new to commentating when he became a member of the America's Cup TV commentating team in San Francisco having spent a distinguished career gathering multiple World, North American and National sailing titles. He made two attempts on the Volvo Ocean Race crown as skipper of PUMA Ocean Racing in 2008-09 and 2011-12 and also raced with PACT 95 during the 1995 America's Cup in San Diego, CA. He helmed Dennis Conner's Stars & Stripes for the 1999-2000 and 2002-03 America's Cup campaigns in Auckland, New Zealand.

Tucker Thompson

American TV presenter and host who will work on all public forms of event delivery for the 35th America's Cup including: TV coverage of all AC events, public presentations and ceremonies, press conferences, video features, AC promotional tour for yacht clubs and related groups.

ARTEMIS RACING
APPOINTS CREWSAVER
AS OFFICIAL SAFETY SUPPLIER FOR THE 35TH AMERICA'S CUP

Crewsaver®

Artemis
Artemis Racing

"We understand the dangers of racing these high performance catamarans at 40+ knots, and the safety of the guys on board is our number one priority which is why Crewsaver are our number one choice for taking on this project"

Artemis Racing's Safety Officer and three times Olympian, Anthony Nossiter

Artemis
Racing

Nautical Terms

Nautical terms can be confusing and off-putting but the only sin greater than not knowing the right term is using the wrong one. Here is a guide to avoid embarrassment.

Port
Left-hand side of boat or a short cut to a monumental headache.

Starboard
Right-hand side of boat not a chart of celestial bodies.

Buoy
Anchored floating device to indicate a position or navigational aid.

Bow
Front of a boat and what is expected if you bump into Royalty.

Stern
Back end of a boat or a skippers expression when you've messed up.

Heel
When a boat is tipped over by the wind

Foil (hydrofoil)
A wing that 'flies' in water and lifts boat out of water at higher speeds.

Sheets
Ropes that pull sails into position, never made from satin and uncomfortable to sleep under.

Grinder
A high powered pedestal-mounted winch for positioning sails or the beefcake operating it.

Lay-line
Straight line a boat can take without altering course to clear a mark or obstacle.

Windward
The direction the wind is blowing from.

Leeward
The direction the wind is blowing towards.

Gybe
Turning a boat through the wind while sailing away from it.

Tack
Turning the boat through the wind while sailing into it.

Flood tide
Tide coming in.

Ebb tide
Tide going out.

Slack tide
In-between tide not one that struggles to get out of bed.

Cover
Legally obstructing or blocking an opponent so they cannot out-manoeuvre you.

Gate
Space between two marks that boats must pass through but tricky to open.

Hike
No legs required just big bottoms to sit on rail and keep boat from heeling.

Leg
A section of the course.

THE BEST SAILORS IN THE WORLD
THE FASTEST BOATS ON THE PLANET

LOUIS VUITTON AMERICA'S CUP WORLD SERIES

The Louis Vuitton America's Cup World Series was designed to introduce high drama sailing to a massive new audience around the globe.

The inaugural event was rolled out in 2011 and led up to the 34th America's Cup two years later, with 10 teams racing in identical AC45 catamarans. All the teams claimed they intended to compete in the larger AC72s in San Francisco in 2013 though only three teams Artemis, Luna Rossa and Emirates Team New Zealand actually did.

The AC45s were onedesign wingsail catamarans similar to the fleet of

AC45Fs in action here in Portsmouth but without foils. They were designed to showcase the speeds and manoeuvrability of the boats, which were incredibly difficult to sail, as well as the skills of the sailors.

Identical boats that went faster than the wind required the crews to be strong and fit and it soon became obvious AC45 racing was a young man's game.

Short and compact racing courses were laid just yards from the shore in a radical departure from normal America's Cup racing formats. And the series was a mix of match/fleet race with a few speed trials against the

clock were thrown in with nine events held in Europe and the USA between 2011 and 2013 with the first ever event staged in Cascais in Portugal.

Each race took around 15 minutes and the format was geared towards a winner takes all fleet race, covered live on YouTube.

Emirates Team New Zealand and Oracle Team USA dominated the first three events in 2011 but Italy's two boat Luna Rossa campaign with Piranha and Swordfish and Artemis Racing's White and Red from Sweden came knocking soon after with Energy Team from France and Team Korea. Land Rover BAR joined the series in 2013.

LOUIS VUITTON

AMERICA'S CUP

WORLD SERIES

PREVIOUS ACWS EVENTS

2011
Cascais, Portugal
Plymouth, UK
San Diego, USA

2012
Naples, Italy
Venice, Italy
Newport, USA
San Francisco, August, USA
San Francisco, October, USA

2013
Naples, Italy

THE 2015 LOUIS VUITTON
AMERICA'S CUP WORLD SERIES
WILL OPEN IN PORTSMOUTH
FROM 23 TO 26 JULY THEN MOVE
TO GOTHENBURG FROM 28 TO
30 AUGUST, 2015 AND BERMUDA
FROM 16 TO 18 OCTOBER, 2015

GOTHENBURG

Thanks to Torbjörn Törnqvist, billionaire founder and owner of the Artemis team, the top specialists in crewed inshore racing will be able to lap up the delights of late summer in this southern Swedish city on a well-protected race zone. Racing will take place either on the Gota River close to the city centre or at Långedrag and the race village, AC Park, will be in Frihamnen. "It's super exciting to announce that the America's Cup World Series is coming to Sweden. It will provide a great opportunity for Artemis Racing to showcase our sport and our America's Cup program" said Iain Percy, the British double Olympic gold medallist and Artemis Racing's Team Manager.

BERMUDA

Bermuda is celebrated in the international sailing community as the finish port for the Newport-Bermuda race, which will celebrate its 50th edition next year and for the Bermuda Gold Cup, the oldest one-design match racing event in the world, dating back to 1937. Now, the island is set to host one of the opening events in the competition for the America's Cup, the oldest trophy in international sport and in 2017, the America's Cup Challenger finals and the final itself. Between Hamilton and Somerset Village, sheltered from the coral reefs, the crews will fly across its translucent, turquoise waters, enabling media and guests to watch racing in an exceptional ambiance and setting.

The 2016 America's Cup World Series will comprise between four and six events including second events in Portsmouth and Bermuda as well as a regatta in Chicago during the summer.

BERMUDA
HOME OF THE 35TH AMERICA'S CUP 2017

AMERICA'S CUP
BERMUDA
—— 2017 ——

THE NEXT AMERICA'S CUP WILL BE CONTESTED IN BERMUDA IN 2017 AFTER DEFENDING CHAMPIONS ORACLE TEAM USA CHOSE THE TINY MID-ATLANTIC ISLAND AS HOST OF THE WORLD'S OLDEST SPORTS TROPHY

Competing against San Francisco and then San Diego, it was the British overseas territory, that put in the winning bid making it the first time ever that the Cup will be defended by an American team outside America.

For over three centuries, the mystique surrounding Bermuda has been slowly evolving, with each generation adding its own tales to the story.

The first known European explorer to reach Bermuda was Spanish sea captain Juan de Bermúdez in 1503, after whom the islands are named.

The archipelago is composed of 181 islands, totalling 21 square miles, and has just over 60,000 residents and, as you would expect in a place with so many islands, water activities are its' life-blood.

Familiar as a stopover for large ocean liners the archipelago has a long record as a sailing venue, hosting international events like the prestigious Newport–Bermuda Yacht Race and the Bermuda Gold Cup. It also gave its name to the Bermudan rig, the typical sail configuration for most modern sailboats.

Celebrated for crystal blue water and beautiful pink sand beaches, Bermuda's Great Sound will form a natural amphitheatre for the race course while the planned America's Cup Village at the Royal Naval Dockyard, will be the beating heart of the America's Cup experience.

Featuring all the team bases, a pit row, food and beverage stalls, entertainment and concerts, the America's Cup Village will be a great destination for hard-core America's Cup fans, or any sporting tourist for that matter. Moreover, historical wind data indicate there should be racing excellent conditions 90% of the time in June.

The America's Cup competitors have agreed the format for June 2017 with all racing taking place on the waters of the Great Sound. All teams will compete in a double round robin format for the Louis Vuitton America's Cup Qualifiers, which will be sailed in the new AC Class foiling catamaran.

The top four challengers from the Louis Vuitton America's Cup Qualifiers will advance to the Challenger Playoffs which consist of a match racing semi-final and finals. The winner of the Playoffs will meet the defending champion, ORACLE TEAM USA, in the 35th America's Cup Match presented by Louis Vuitton.

HAVE YOU BEEN INSPIRED BY THE ACWS SAILING AND FANCY GETTING OUT ON THE WATER?

You too can enjoy the freedom, exhilaration and adventure of sailing

IT REALLY IS A SPORT FOR ALL!

R⅄A

DINGHIES

Dinghy sailing is one of the easiest and most affordable ways to get on the water. In these fun, small boats you can sail on your own or with friends and family. There's no better way to get a feel for sailing a boat and its interaction with the wind and water. Easy to transport and set-up, dinghies can be sailed by people of all ages, fitness levels and abilities.

YACHTING

If you're interested in bigger boats, yacht sailing is extremely diverse, sociable and enjoyable, whether you want to relax, cruising with friends or family, or get the adrenaline buzz of racing with your crew. Every experience offers a unique adventure and there are a huge variety of tasks onboard – from controlling the sails to helming or navigating.

WINDSURFING

Windsurfing combines elements of surfing and sailing, and can be as sedate or extreme as you wish it to be. Speeds of up to 30 mph are ultimately achievable and there is no greater thrill than skimming across the surface of the water with family, friends or newly found windsurfing buddies.

HOW MUCH DOES IT COST?

Sailing has always been presumed to be an expensive sport, but the reality is that it doesn't have to be!

Clubs and training centres hold regular open days and taster sessions for you to 'have a go' usually for free or at a very low cost. You don't need any equipment initially as you can join a club for as little as £150 per annum (cheaper than most gyms!) with many offering boats to hire or borrow for free whilst you develop your skills. Many sailors don't end up owning their own boat because those who do are often looking for crew! Additionally after initial training equipment can be hired from most recognised training centres.

If you do want to get your own gear, you can buy a small dinghy for as little as £500 and a wetsuit will cost around £70. RYA Training is recommend but once you know the basics, the cost of riding the wind and waves is free, so go for it!

To find all the information you need to start your sailing adventure visit www.rya.org.uk/startboating

St Paul's Catholic Primary School
Bourne Road
Portsmouth
Hampshire
PO6 4JD

(02392) 375488

admin@st-pauls.portsmouth.sch.uk

ST PAUL'S CATHOLIC PRIMARY SCHOOL AND NURSERY

'Do everything with love'

First letter of St Paul to the Corinthians 16:14

This is a Good school

OFSTED 2015

Vacancies available for September 2015

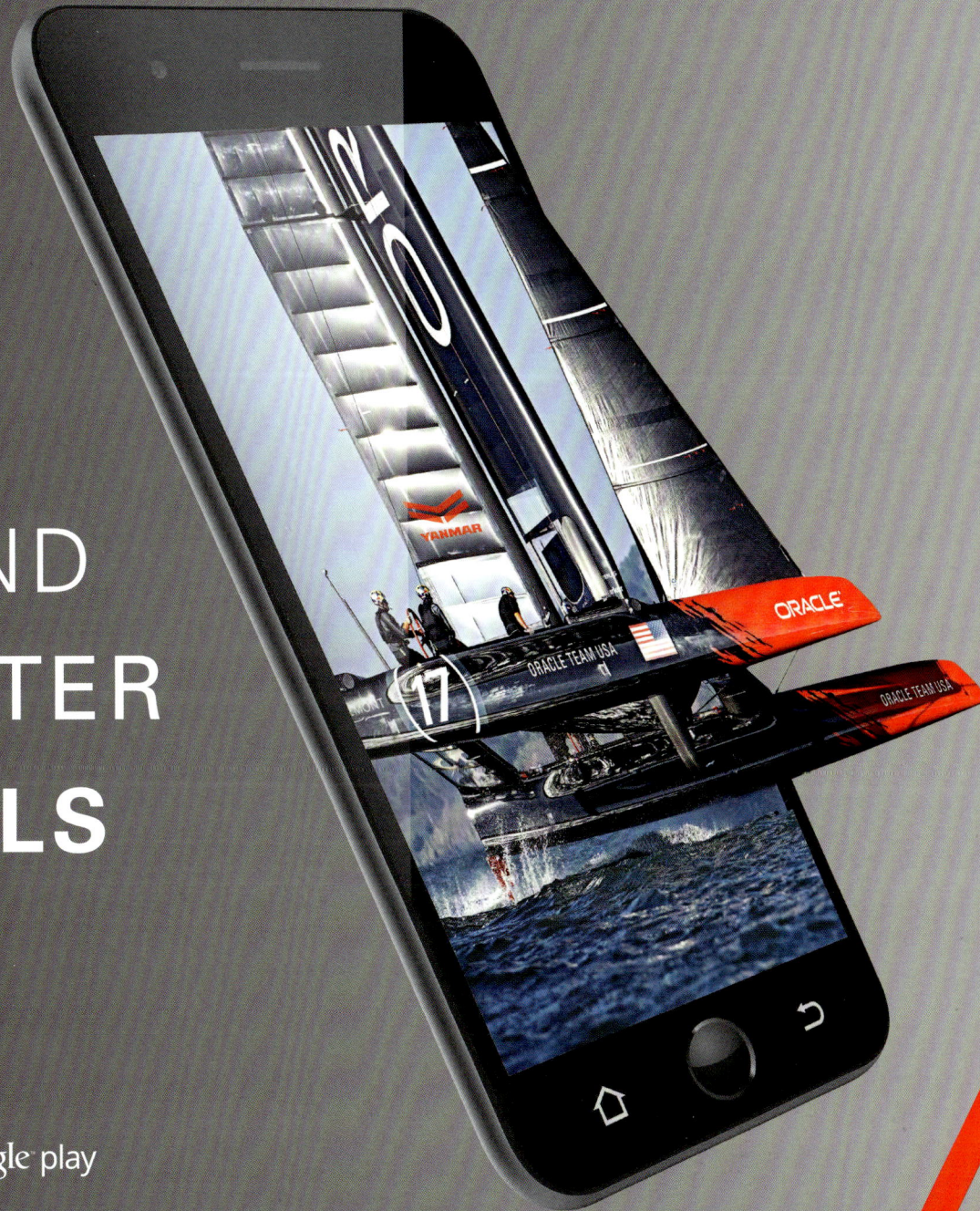

THE OFFICIAL MOBILE APP OF THE AMERICA'S CUP

WIND
WATER
FOILS

Download the app on
 App Store | Google play

'Volunteers are the heart of any big sports event, they engage local people who are passionate about their city'

I f you saw a happy smiley face as you walked into the Louis Vuitton America's Cup World Series village who came to your rescue when you were wondering where to go or what to do, chances are they were a Wavemaker.

Or if you ventured out on a dayboat to watch the AC45Fs hurtle down the Solent but weren't sure where the race track started, a Wavemaker would almost certainly have had the answer and delivered it with a smile.

Since February this year, ACWS Portsmouth organisers Team Origin have been recruiting local volunteers to help make the event go as smoothly as previous large scale events staged in Portsmouth.

Remember 2008 when around 200,000 Pompey fans turned out for the FA Cup winning celebration parade. Or 2012 when 50,000 people came to Southsea Common to see the Olympic Torch pass through.

This weekend, we are likely to see 500,000 visitors to Portsmouth, many of whom will never have visited the city before and almost certainly will never have attended a sailing event.

So around 250 enthusiastic Wavemakers landside and the 60 extra volunteers in around 40 boats on the water, all of whom are local to the area, will explain from a variety of volunteer stations, including all the park and ride sites, transport hubs, big screen sites, the Fanzone and Waterfront arenas, what is going on and where it is happening.

"Volunteers are the heart of any big sports event, they engage local people who are passionate about their city," said Wavemaker coordinator Geoff Terry, who received applications from keen potential volunteers in Russia, Sweden, Japan, Spain and France.

"The idea is that all our visitors turn up with a smile and leave with a bigger one so our Wavemakers will be full of knowledge, information, and enthusiasm.

"We have found people who are keen to make sure that all event visitors have an amazing and unforgettable experience.

All volunteers, recognisable by their red Wavemaker cap, T-shirts and waterproofs, were fully-trained and assigned to different roles, giving them the opportunity to be part of a world class event over four days, and play their own part in a slice of British sporting history.

'We have found people who are keen to make sure that all event visitors have an amazing and unforgettable experience '

RAPIER 550
PERFORMANCE CATAMARAN

We have taken a new look at fast cruising and the 550 brings together an incredible combination of high performance, high specification and radical new design. The 550 is a new generation of innovative, beautiful, high performance catamarans with a true racing heritage, giving class-leading performance. Intelligent electronics navigation and radically simple sail handling is standard, as are creative, contemporary and luxury interiors.

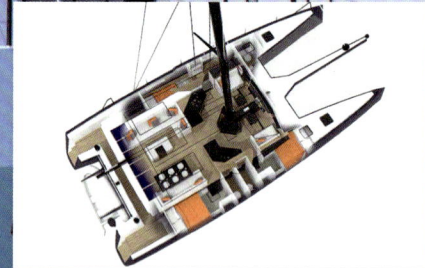

- Cruising speeds in excess of 15 knots and over 300 miles per day, giving shorter passage times and ability to more easily avoid adverse weather conditions.
- Easy and safe single handed sailing capability - everything is controlled from a single place, inside.
- Designed for long distance cruising, not a converted charter boat - low maintenance, higher quality, better performance, longer life.
- Huge entertaining space.
- Semi custom build to better match owners planned sailing agenda.

Awards: Best catamaran in the 2015 European Yacht of the Year Competition - Blue Water Cruiser category.

Tel: +44 (0) 333 600 2603 | sales@broadblue.com | www.broadblue.com

destination
PORTSMOUTH

Over the past decade, Portsmouth has undergone a transformation from being the hub of Britain's naval operations to playing a different role as one of the country's fastest developing and dynamic business, tourism and cultural centres.

Towering over this great waterfront city is the Emirates Spinnaker Tower opened in 2005 as the centrepiece of the Renaissance of Portsmouth Harbour Project which stands 110m high with two viewing decks at the top, one with a glass floor for intrepid explorers!

At its base, Gunwharf Quays comprises more than 90 premium outlet stores to cater for all fashion tastes and budgets plus another 30 bars and restaurants from coffee and cake to haute cuisine. At the heart of the city is the Portsmouth Historic Dockyard, home to the finest maritime heritage in the world showcasing 800 years of naval history within working docks and historic buildings.

This is the only place in the world where visitors can experience first-hand what it was like to serve and fight on board the ships that shaped Britain's history - alongside contemporary warships of the Royal Navy.

Along the Millennium Promenade and the cobbled streets of Old Portsmouth offer a mix of old and new with the Cathedral, Garrison Church and historic fortifications lying side by side the stunning new HQ for Land Rover BAR. Located on the seafront at Southsea, the D-Day Museum is Britain's only museum dedicated solely to the D-Day landings in Normandy, France in 1944 and Southsea Castle, built by Henry VIII 400 years earlier in 1544. Charles Dickens was born in Portsmouth and his family home has been preserved as a museum.

Sherlock Holmes was also 'conceived' in the city since it was where his creator Sir Arthur Conan Doyle lived and practiced medicine.

Portsmouth's past is rich in colour and action and the future looks fascinating too. Last year, the first ever joint city deal was announced, which saw Portsmouth awarded £50m of government funding to unlock a £900m strategic development site at Tipner, the gateway to the city with the potential for a massive 2,370 new homes and 3,600 new jobs.

The Naval Base will also benefit from £100m of infrastructure development ahead of the arrival of the Queen Elizabeth Class Aircraft Carriers. Significant improvements to the city's road network, a purpose-built public transport interchange, a brand new University Technical College and plans to find space for a 5-star hotel will all ensure the Portsmouth tradition continues to thrive, with all guns blazing.

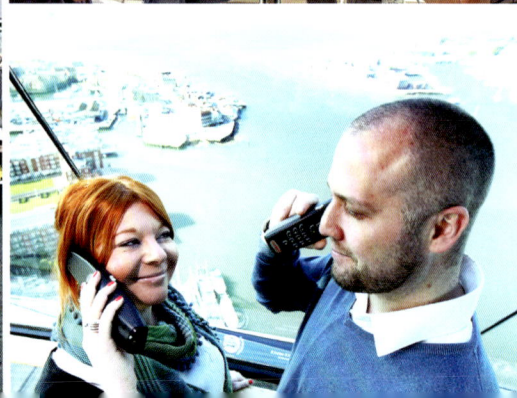

VIEW THINGS DIFFERENTLY

EXPLORE 3 VIEW DECKS WITH 350° PANORAMIC VIEWS

- ❯ i-VIEW INTERACTIVE VIEW INTERPRETATION SCREENS
- ❯ BREATHTAKING GLASS SKY WALK
- ❯ HIGH SPY INTERACTIVE SHIP FINDER
- ❯ AUDIO GUIDES (CHILD FRIENDLY AND MULTIPLE LANGUAGE VERSIONS AVAILABLE)
- ❯ OPEN AIR SKY DECK
- ❯ CAFÉ IN THE CLOUDS OFFERING HOT & COLD DRINKS AND SNACKS

PLUS WATERFRONT CAFÉ

- ❯ BEAUTIFUL MARINA VIEWS AND TERRACE
- ❯ SERVING DELICIOUS DRINKS, SNACKS AND HOT & COLD FOOD

SPECIAL PACKAGE
24TH – 26TH JULY: ENTRANCE, SOUVENIR PHOTO AND GUIDEBOOK PLUS GLASS OF PROSECCO - £26PP

GUNWHARF QUAYS, PORTSMOUTH PO1 3TT
02392 857520

WWW.SPINNAKERTOWER.CO.UK

A great day out...Don't miss it

The Mary Rose Museum

The exciting new £27 million Mary Rose Museum opened in May 2013 and offers one of the most significant insights into Tudor life anywhere in the world from the 20,000 artefacts that lay at the bottom of the Solent for more than 400 years after Henry VIII's warship sank in 1545.

HMS Warrior 1860

The only surviving member of Queen Victoria's Black Battle Fleet, Warrior was launched in 1860, and was the pride of the Queen's fleet. Powered by steam and sail, she was the largest, fastest and most powerful ship of her day and had a profound influence on naval architecture.

The National Museum of the Royal Navy

One of the country's leading maritime museums devoted to the ships of the Royal Navy and the men and women who served on board and featuring. Hear My Story, a major £4.5m exhibition telling the undiscovered stories from those who have played a part in the Royal Navy's history.

New for 2015 – Opens August

The Royal Navy's HMS M.33 was launched in May 1915 and is the sole remaining British survivor of that year's bloody Gallipoli Campaign. She is the only British warship from the First World War to be open to the public during the centenary year

HMS Victory

Now in the custodianship of the National Museum of the Royal Navy, Nelson's flagship is undergoing a period of restoration and visitors have a unique opportunity to witness the 'facelift' of the oldest commissioned warship in the world.

She's a proud memorial to Vice Admiral Lord Horatio Nelson, Britain's greatest Naval hero and his victory at the Battle of Trafalgar in 1805. During the fight Nelson was mortally wounded and is now remembered as one of Britain's greatest war heroes.

No English ships were destroyed in the battle but Nelson was amongst the 1,500 English Seamen that were killed or wounded.

Across the water

The Royal Navy Submarine Museum, located at Gosport, tells the story of the Royal Navy's submarine service and is home to the Royal Navy's very first submarine Holland 1 and the only surviving WW2 era submarines remaining in the UK, the mighty HMS Alliance and midget X24.

Explosion Museum of Naval Firepower

Explosion Museum of Naval Firepower Award winning museum of naval warfare created within 18th century buildings at the Royal Navy's former armaments depot at Priddy's Hard, in Gosport, Hampshire.

Harbour Tour

The 45 minute Harbour Tour takes visitors around Portsmouth Harbour and the Naval Dockyard providing unrivalled views of the modern Royal Navy, historical sights and areas of the Solent coastline.

In Portsmouth the world's best sailors compete for the ultimate prize, to become the official Challenger for the America's Cup.

On behalf of the City, I'd like to welcome all the teams and spectators for what promises to be a sensational few days. Over the four day event you will witness exhilarating racing from the best sailors in the world, on the most advanced craft. The action will unfold along the stunning and historic Southsea waterfront which affords excellent views of the racing.

The organisers have arranged a fantastic event where you can enjoy a festival atmosphere on and off the water, as the seafront is transformed into an entertainment arena. Undeniably, the races themselves will create a real buzz throughout the city. Congratulations to Sir Keith Mills and Team Origin who had the vision to deliver such a high-calibre event. And my huge thanks to all the stakeholders who brought together this truly city-wide partnership.

There are also long-term benefits from the Louis Vuitton America's Cup Series, boosting the region's economy, attracting more maritime and marine industries and showing off the city's wider potential. The event will also encourage the next generation of world-class sailors, designers and engineers, inspired by watching futuristic AC45 foiling catamarans launch out of the water.

I'm bound to be biased, but there's no better city in the world to host this fantastic event. We can't guarantee the finest weather but you can expect the warmest of welcomes. Whilst I hope to be cheering Sir Ben and his team right through to bringing the world's oldest sporting trophy home to Britain, I wish all the teams good luck and good sailing.

Cllr Donna Jones
Leader of Portsmouth City Council

FIRST
THURSDAY
23RD JULY 2015

AMERICA'S CUP
WORLD SERIES
PORTSMOUTH

DAYTIME ACTION 10AM – 5PM:

- SCHOOLS OUT/KIDS ZONE
- BE THE FIRST TO SEE THE ACTION
- THE CUP COMES TO TOWN
- OFFICIAL PARADE OF SAIL
- WORLD CLASS SAILORS
- BEN AINSLIE RACING FEATURE AREA
- LOCAL LIVE BANDS
- VARIETY OF EXHIBITS
- AMAZING FOOD AND BAR OFFERINGS
- FULL ON STAGE PROGRAMME
- LIVE MCS & COMMENTARY
- OFFICIAL PRESS CONFERENCE

EVENING PROGRAMME:

PORTSMOUTH *Live*

SOUTH COAST PROMS

EVENT OPENING CEREMONY & SOUTH COAST PROMS 2015

featuring The Massed Bands of Her Majesty's Royal Marines

FOR MORE INFORMATION VISIT: WWW.TICKETMASTER.CO.UK/ACWSPORTSMOUTH
WWW.ACWSPORTSMOUTH.COM

DAY ONE

THURSDAY 23RD JULY

Thursday is all about a series of 'Firsts' hence why we called it 'First Thursday' – make sure you are one of the first people to be there when the show comes to town and see for yourself what all the fuss is about. Its also the first day of school holidays for everyone – 'Schools out – summer's here!

See below planned activities for the day and evening:

0900-1100	The race teams and boats get ready in the Naval Base – come and view in the Historic Dockyard
1000	Race Village opens on Southsea Common and the day programme kicks off
1100	The America's Cup 'trophy' arrives in style
1115-1230	Moth racing and kitesurfing displays
1230	The Official Parade of Sail leaves the Royal Navy base and escorts the race fleet out to the race course area in front of the race village on Southsea Common
1245-1430	Official Parade of Sail and exhibition sailing by the race teams
1500	Skippers come ashore
1515	Official press conference & presentation of skippers in Fanzone Arena
1700	Day programme ends
1830	Evening programme opens
1900-1945	Official Opening Ceremony
2000-2200	South Coast Proms concert featuring The Massed Bands of Her Majesty's Royal Marines

Programme subject to change

DAY TWO

FRIDAY 24TH JULY

Friday focuses on the 'speed' – everything is flying from the race boats to the Red Arrows to F1 features. Lots of thrills and spills and drama in store, a great day to get away from the City and come to the seaside.

See below planned activities for the day and evening:

0900-1100	The race teams and boats get ready in the Naval Base – come and view in the Historic Dockyard
1000	Race Village opens on Southsea Common and the day programme kicks off
1100 -1200	Moth racing and kitesurfing displays
1210-1232	Red Arrows display
1230	The race boats leave the Royal Navy base and are escorted to the race course area in front of the race village on Southsea Common
1245-1320	Race boats tuning up before practice racing with live MC commentary
1330-1500	Practise starts and two practise races
1515	Skippers come ashore
1530	Media mixed zone with skippers in Fanzone Arena
1700	Day programme ends
1830	Evening programme opens
1915-2130	South Coast Proms concert featuring The Massed Bands of Her Majesty's Royal Marines

Day and evening tickets available on www.ticketmaster.co.uk/acwsportsmouth

---

AMERICA'S CUP WORLD SERIES PORTSMOUTH

FAST FRIDAY
24TH JULY 2015

DAYTIME ACTION 10AM - 5PM:

- FLYING ACTION
- F1 AND AMERICA'S CUP COMPARISON
- DESIGN AND TECHNOLOGY FEATURES
- RED ARROWS DISPLAY
- PRACTISE STARTS
- PREVIEW RACING ACTION
- LOCAL LIVE BANDS
- VARIETY OF EXHIBITS
- AMAZING FOOD AND BAR OFFERINGS
- ROYAL MARINES DISPLAY
- LIVE MCS & COMMENTARY
- SKIPPERS PARADE AFTER SAILING

EVENING PROGRAMME:

PORTSMOUTH *Live*

SOUTH COAST PROMS

SOUTH COAST PROMS 2015
featuring The Massed Bands of Her Majesty's Royal Marines

FOR MORE INFORMATION VISIT: WWW.TICKETMASTER.CO.UK/ACWSPORTSMOUTH
WWW.ACWSPORTSMOUTH.COM

BIG SATURDAY
25TH JULY 2015

AMERICA'S CUP WORLD SERIES PORTSMOUTH

DAYTIME ACTION 10AM - 5PM:

- SAILING GETS SERIOUS
- POINTS ON THE SCOREBOARD
- OFFICIAL RACING STARTS
- AERIAL DISPLAYS
- LOCAL LIVE BANDS
- VARIETY OF EXHIBITS
- CLOSE UP VIEW OF THE RACE BOATS
- AMAZING FOOD AND BAR OFFERINGS
- ROYAL MARINES LANDING CRAFT DISPLAY
- FULL ON STAGE PROGRAMME
- LIVE MCS & COMMENTARY
- SKIPPERS PARADE AFTER SAILING

EVENING PROGRAMME:

PORTSMOUTH Live

LINE UP INCLUDES:
SPANDAU BALLET, WET WET WET MCBUSTED & CARLY RAE JEPSEN

line up subject to change

FOR MORE INFORMATION VISIT: WWW.TICKETMASTER.CO.UK/ACWSPORTSMOUTH
WWW.ACWSPORTSMOUTH.COM

DAY THREE

SATURDAY 25TH JULY

Big Saturday says it all – today sailing gets serious and points are won or lost. The full official racing of the 35th America's Cup kicks off today so lets all get involved and support our favourite team! As with the other days, the programme is action packed for both the day and evening so make it a date!
See below planned activities for the day and evening:

0900-1100	The race teams and boats get ready in the Naval Base – come and view in the Historic Dockyard
1000	Race Village opens on Southsea Common and the day programme kicks off
1030	RNLI helicopter display
1100-1230	Moth racing and kitesurfing displays
1200	Red Bull Matador air display
1230	The race boats leave the Royal Navy base and are escorted to the race course area in front of the race village on Southsea Common
1245-1320	Race boats tuning up before racing with live MC commentary
1330-1500	Two races
1515	Skippers come ashore
1530	Skippers in media mixed zone in Fanzone Arena
1600	Blades air display
1700	Day programme ends
1800	Evening programme opens
1900-2300	Portsmouth Live! Saturday day concert featuring Spandau Ballet, Wet Wet Wet, McBusted and Carly Rae Jepsen

Programme subject to change

DAY FOUR

SUNDAY 26TH JULY

Sunday is guaranteed to be 'super' – a fantastic finale to the event where the overall winner will be decided through what is sure to be some nail biting racing. As ever a full programme of entertainment on shore and on water and then an amazing prizegiving gala event to end it all.

See below planned activities for the day and evening:

0900-1100	The race teams and boats get ready in the Naval Base – come and view in the Historic Dockyard
1000	Race Village opens on Southsea Common and the day programme kicks off
1030	RNLI helicopter display
1100-1230	Moth racing and kitesurfing displays
1200	Trig aerial display
1230	The race boats leave the Royal Navy base and are escorted to the race course area in front of the race village on Southsea Common
1245-1320	Race boats tuning up before racing with live MC commentary
1330-1500	Two races (double points)
1515	Skippers come ashore
1530	Skippers in media mixed zone in Fanzone Arena
1600	All skippers and sailors to main stage in Waterfront Festival Arena
1615-1700	Gala prizegiving event in main stage in Waterfront Festival Arena
1800	Day programme & event end

Day and evening tickets available on www.ticketmaster.co.uk/acwsportsmouth

SUPER SUNDAY
26TH JULY 2015

AMERICA'S CUP WORLD SERIES PORTSMOUTH

DAYTIME ACTION 10AM - 6PM:

- WINNER TAKES ALL
- DOUBLE POINTS RACING
- AERIAL DISPLAYS
- RUNNERS AND RIDERS
- LOCAL LIVE BANDS
- VARIETY OF EXHIBITS
- AMAZING FOOD AND BAR OFFERINGS
- FULL ON STAGE PROGRAMME
- LIVE MCS & COMMENTARY
- SKIPPERS PARADE AFTER SAILING
- OFFICIAL PRIZEGIVING ON MAIN STAGE
- SPECIAL GUEST APPEARANCES

AFTER RACING : OFFICIAL PRIZEGIVING:

SPECIAL GUEST APPEARANCES
OFFICIAL PRIZE GIVING EVENT

FOR MORE INFORMATION VISIT: WWW.TICKETMASTER.CO.UK/ACWSPORTSMOUTH
WWW.ACWSPORTSMOUTH.COM

LOUIS VUITTON
AMERICA'S CUP
WORLD SERIES
— PORTSMOUTH —

WATERFRONT FESTIVAL ARENA

1. CHILDREN'S ZONE
2. EXHIBITS
3. WATERFRONT BAR
4. MAIN STAGE & SCREENS
5. WATERFRONT BAR

6. BEN AINSLIE RACING/1851 TRUST
7. BIG WHEEL
8. RETAIL & EXHIBITS
9. GUINNESS BAR
10. WATERFRONT BAR

11. WATERFRONT BAR
12. BEACH DISPLAY / LANDING AREA
13. RACE VIEWING AREAS
14. AC MERCHANDISE
15. FOOD & DRINK

X
ENTRANCES / EXITS

TOILETS

MEDICAL CENT

INFO POINT

WELFARE
LOST CHILDRE

E1

LIFEGUARD

MOZARELLA JOES

LIFEGUARD

PRE-PAID PARKING

WATERFRONT FESTIVAL ARENA

E2

E5

E3

BLUE REEF AQUARIUM

THE RACE TRACK

ACCESS TO FANZONE & VIP HOSPITALITY

AMERICA'S CUP WORLD SERIES — PORTSMOUTH

WATERFRONT FESTIVAL ARENA

THE THEME OF THIS EVENT IS 'SOMETHING FOR EVERYONE'. THE **WATERFRONT FESTIVAL ARENA** TAKES UP THE MAJORITY OF SOUTHSEA COMMON AND IS A FREE TO VIEW AREA DURING THE DAY WHERE SPECTATORS WILL FIND A FULL PROGRAMME OF FAMILY FRIENDLY ACTIVITIES

A large hosted stage, big screens, local bands, food and beverage concessions, an array of exhibits and displays and a prime view of the on water action.

The day programme runs from Thursday 23rd to Sunday 26th July and the kicks off at 1000 each day running through to 1700. There is a massive stage and two enormous screens where the live hosts will fill the day with a schedule to suit all tastes. Everything from stunning aerial displays, inteviews on stage, games for the kids, interactive displays, local bands to entertain...and then of course the on water action with the flying 'Moths' and kitesurfers each morning and the AC45 race boats and teams on the water each day from 1230.

Plenty to eat and drink too with a wide range of cool bars and food outlets, lots of space to spread out your blanket and take in the rays and the view.

The evening programme runs from the main stage on Thursday 23rd 1830 – 2200 with the opening Ceremony and South Coast Proms first night (Massed Bands of Her Majesty's Royal Marines), Friday 24th 1830 – 2200 2nd night of the South Coast Proms and the Big Saturday night 25th July (pre-bar opens at 1700, gates open at 1800 - 2300) for the Portsmouth Live! Concert line-up with Spandau Ballet, Wet Wet Wet, Mc Busted and Carly Rae Jepsen – don't miss out and book your tickets!

And to top it all, make sure you check out the range of exhibitors and experience the variety of activities on display.

EXHIBITORS*

- LAND ROVER BAR & 1851 TRUST
- AMERICA'S CUP CINEMA EXPERIENCE
- ANDREW SIMPSON SAILING FOUNDATION
- BIG WHEEL FEATURE
- BMW
- BRITISH CANOE ASSOCIATION
- CLIPPER
- FACE PAINTING
- GOSLINGS RUM BAR/DARK & STORMY DECK
- GUINNESS BAR
- HAMPSHIRE FIRE & RESCUE
- HEART FM
- AMERICA'S CUP MERCHANDISING STORES
- KIDS ZONE WITH LASER QUEST
- KING'S THEATRE
- PLAY BUS
- PORTSMOUTH MUSEUM
- PORTSMOUTH WATERSPORTS CENTRE
- RED BULL
- RNLI
- ROYAL NAVY & ROYAL MARINES
- ROYAL YACHTING ASSOCIATION
- SOUTHERN WATER
- THE NEWS
- TOTS PLAY AREA
- VISIT PORTSMOUTH
- WAITROSE
- WATERFRONT BARS
- YAMAHA
- ZORBING

*Exhibitors list correct at time of going to press.

FANZONE ARENA & VIP HOSPITALITY AREA

1. GRANDSTAND SEATING
2. EXHIBITS
3. EXCLUSIVE VIEWING AREAS
4. BANDSTAND FEATURE BAR
5. STAGE & BIG SCREEN
6. INFO BRANDING
7. DISABLED ACCESS PLATFORM
8. FOOD CONCESSIONS & RETAIL
9. AC MERCHANDISE & EXHIBITS
10. THE FANZONE BAR

X
ENTRANCES / EXITS

TOILETS

MEDICAL CENTRE

INFO POINT

LOUIS VUITTON
AMERICA'S CUP
WORLD SERIES
— PORTSMOUTH —

VIP PARKING

VIP PARKING ZONE

VIP & MEDIA SHUTTLE BUSES

E4

TV / MEDIA COMPOUND

VIP HOSPITALITY PAVILION

E5

THE RACE TRACK

FANZONE ARENA

WATERFRONT PAVILION

AMERICA'S CUP WORLD SERIES — PORTSMOUTH —

AMERICA'S CUP WORLD SERIES — PORTSMOUTH —

THE TICKETED **FANZONE ARENA** CATERS FOR THOSE WHO WANT TO IMMERSE THEMSELVES IN THE WORLD OF AMERICA'S CUP. AN AREA DEDICATED TO THOSE WHO WANT TO LEARN ALL ABOUT THE SPORT, THE SAILORS, THE TECHNOLOGY, THE RACING, THE HISTORY OF THE CUP, THE RUNNERS AND RIDERS AND HOW IT ALL WORKS

A staged programme throughout the day featuring the live racing with expert commentary and hosts and a range of additional features guaranteed to keep the attention of the most excited fan!

The Fanzone Arena also houses a ticketed grandstand for 1500 and the amazing **VIP HOSPITALITY WATERFRONT PAVILION** for the truly best seats in the house. The Arena has a high bank running all around the back to give fantastic views as well as an exclusive promenade literally metres away from the leeward gate of the race course.

Also to be found in the Fanzone Arena is the Media Centre and TV compound – making sure we all have the news and action when we want it and where we need it!

The day programme runs from Thursday 23rd to Sunday 26th July and the kicks off at 1000 each day running through to 1800. There is a feature stage and big screen where the live hosts will fill the day with a schedule to engage this focused audience. Each day includes everything from stunning aerial displays, key interviews on stage, interactive displays and of course the on water action with the flying 'Moths' and kitesurfers each morning and the AC45 race boats and teams on the water each day from 1230.

EXHIBITORS*

- LAND ROVER BAR FEATURE WITH NACRA TRAINING BOAT
- BERMUDA TOURISM AUTHORITY
- BREMONT WATCHES
- BMW
- FANZONE BARS AND FOOD CONCESSIONS
- GOSLINGS RUM
- HYDRO POOLS
- MOET ET CHANDON CHAMPAGNE TERRACE

*Exhibitors list correct at time of going to press.

THE RACE COURSE

Course 1: Start – M1(port) – L Gate – W Gate – L Mark(port) – Finish (FIVE Leg Course)
Course 2: Start – M1(port) – L Gate – W Gate – L Gate – W Gate – L Mark(port) –Finish (SEVEN Leg Course)

START SEQUENCE:

5 min - 4 min - 3 min - 2 min - 1min - START.   Flags with 5,4,3,2,1, lowered on each minute in countdown.

* This shows typical course layout for southwesterly wind, the course will be aligned with the prevailing wind

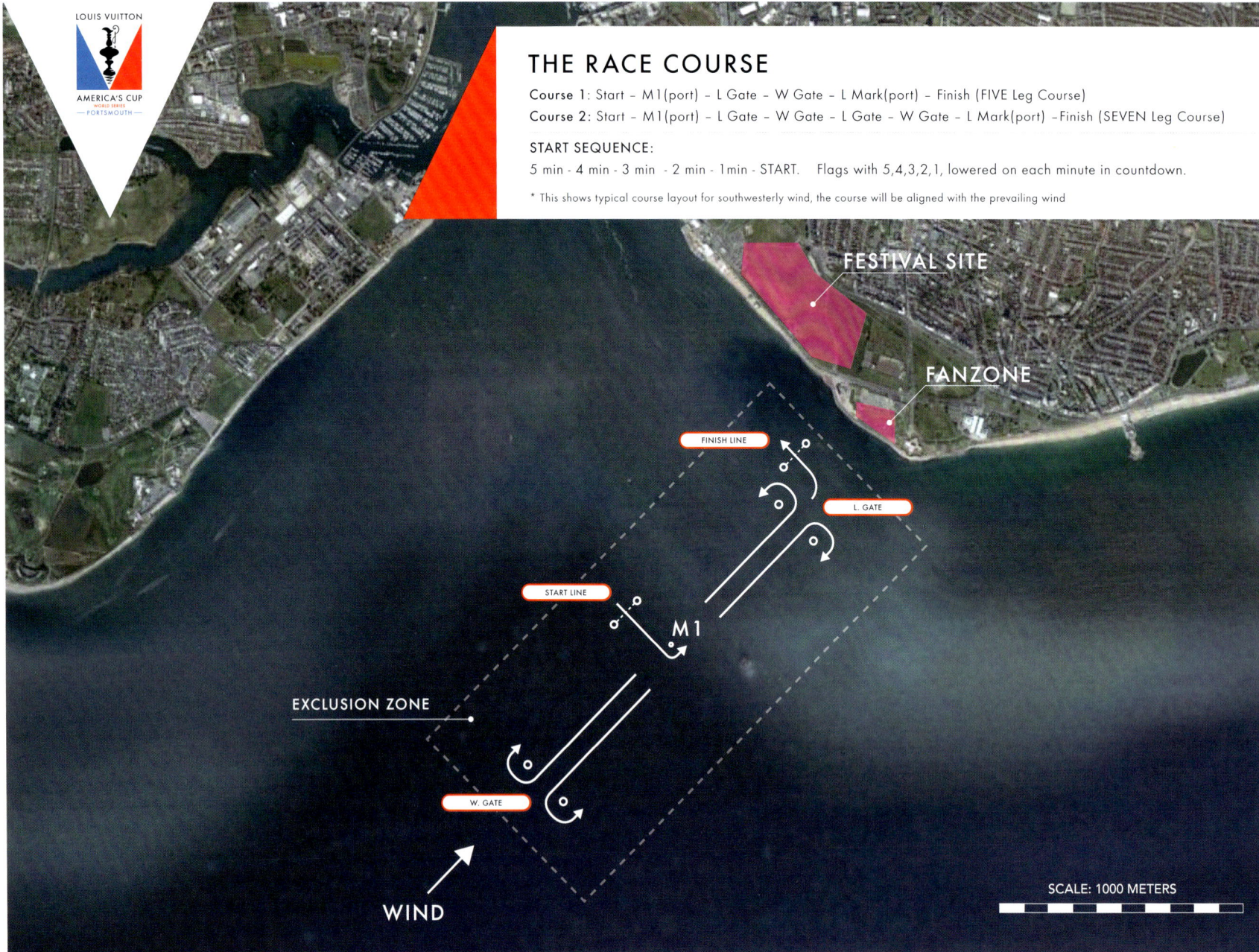

FESTIVAL SITE

FANZONE

FINISH LINE

L. GATE

START LINE

M1

EXCLUSION ZONE

W. GATE

WIND

SCALE: 1000 METERS

Image courtesy of Land Rover BAR

THE RACE COURSE

THE ON WATER RACING ACTION DURING THE LOUIS VUITTON AMERICA'S CUP IS GOING TO BE SPECTACULAR - SITUATED LITERALLY METRES OFF SOUTHSEA COMMON, THIS IS GOING TO BE CENTRE STAGE FOR THE EVENT

The race course is amazingly close to shore but is within a commercial shipping channel and an area managed by the Queen's Harbour Master Portsmouth (QHM).

An exclusion zone will be created around the race course to ensure perfect racing conditions are delivered to the world class sailing teams, but also to ensure the safety of both the racing teams and the spectators – the teams will race in AC45s, foiling catamarans capable of speeds of up to 40 mph!

Given the high speed of the racing catamarans, the arrangements for this event will be extensive, and are primarily focussed on ensuring the safety of competitors, other personnel involved in the racing, spectators and other water users. The racing course will be dependent on the wind direction on each race day and will be refined and published closer to the event in the light of forecast winds. However, in order to illustrate arrangements the attached diagram sets out the plans for the most likely wind at this time of year, a moderate south-westerly.

The full Local Notice to Mariners can be found at: QHM Portsmouth www.royalnavy.mod.uk/qhm/portsmouth/local-notices

The on water and racing programme is as follows:

Thursday 23rd July : 1230 - 1430 : Parade of Sail

Friday 24th July : 1330 - 1500 : Two preview races

Saturday 25th July : 1330 - 1500 : Race 1 and 2

Sunday 26th July : 1330 - 1500 : Race 3 and 4

TRAVEL & DIRECTIONS

The Louis Vuitton America's Cup World Series will be fully signposted over the four days of the event, but here is a little more information about travelling to and from the event here in the Great Waterfront City. Portsmouth is a very well connected city with great public transport routes. We believe this is the best way to travel into the city – you'll be avoiding the traffic and helping the environment!

How do I get to the event?

There are different options for getting to and from the event, as well as getting around in Portsmouth once you're here. Portsmouth City Council's travel advisors and the Louis Vuitton America's Cup World Series Wavemaker volunteers will be on-hand at strategic locations to advise people on the best way to get to the event.

By Air

The nearest airport is Southampton Airport, a mere 22 miles away from Portsmouth with many international flight routes. Taxis are available from Southampton to Portsmouth and car hire also available. Car journey time from Southampton airport to Portsmouth is usually around 30 minutes. Other international airports include London Heathrow (60 miles/100 kms away) and London Gatwick (also 60 miles/100 kms away), hire car or taxi driving time around 1.5 - 2 hours.

By Sea

The event is right by the water after all! Ferry services operate from France, Spain, the Isle of Wight and Gosport on a regular basis – Ferry operators : Brittany Ferries, Wightlink, Hovertravel, Gosport Ferry.

By Rail

There are regular trains from London Waterloo and Victoria Stations, which bring you right into the heart of the waterfront at Portsmouth Harbour Station.

From Portsmouth Harbour Station it's a short 20-minute walk (approx.) Alternatively there are regular buses (see Shuttle buses below) and many taxis in the area that can take you direct to the seafront.

By Coach

There are regular coaches available from London Victoria Coach Station to Portsmouth – many stopping at The Hard Interchange which is home to a bus depot and taxi rank making travel very easy – visit The National Express website for more information.

By Bus

There will be regular shuttle buses running from just outside Portsmouth Harbour train station running to Clarence Pier, right by the Waterfront Festival site – this is a FREE SERVICE. Take Bus number 1 or number 23. Travel by bus around Portsmouth is also very easy with great services provided by Stagecoach and First Group.

On Foot

Portsmouth is a beautiful waterfront city and is very flat! If you are able to walk to the different event hubs we thoroughly recommend taking in the sea air on a lovely walk to the event! Safe walking routes from Portsmouth Harbour Station will be marked 'Follow me' and marshalled by our team of helpful WaveMaker volunteers along the way!

By Bike

Cycling has never been so popular! Why not cycle to the event? There are numerous places around the city with secure bike parking close to the Waterfront Festival site at the Skate Park off Avenue De Caen as well as numerous other places around the city.

Taxis

There will be 2 separate dedicated taxi pick up and drop off points close to the Waterfront Festival site, one on the north side of Clarence Parade for Hackney Cabs and one off Avenue de Caen for Private Hire taxis.

By Road

We are trying to be as green an event as possible - so if you can use public transport, walk or cycle then please do. If you must drive then follow the Highway signs to the appropriate car parks on your way into the city.

There are various options for Parking, as follows:

Park and Ride

There will be additional park and ride car parks for the duration of the Louis Vuitton America's Cup World Series.

Thursday 23rd – Sunday 26th July:

Portsmouth's main park and ride at the Tipner site on the M275 is being supplemented by additional space close by which will benefit from using the infrastructure at the existing Park and Ride. This can be pre-booked by going to www.justpark.com/uk/parking/portsmouth/s/tipner-lane-portsmouth-po2/ for the price of £4, which includes your return bus journey to the event sites.

Saturday – Sunday only:

In addition to the Tipner Park and Ride, there will be an additional park and ride facility at King George V Playing Field near Cosham with regular buses running to the event sites throughout the day, this parking can also be pre-booked by clicking www.justpark.com/uk/parking/portsmouth/s/western-road-portsmouth-po6/ Please note – all park and rides can be paid for on the day, although we do recommend pre-booking where possible.

Pre-booked event parking on Southsea Common

There will be a limited amount of bespoke event parking on Southsea Common, right next to the event site, including some accessible parking (no charge). The car park address is Clarence Parade, Portsmouth PO5 3NU. The cost of this car park is £12 per day (+ booking fee) and can be booked via https://go.justpark.com/SeafrontPortsmouth.

VIP/Accessible Fanzone Parking

If you have a hospitality car pass or if you are a Blue Badge holder with a Fanzone ticket, please follow signs to the "VIP car park" close to Southsea Castle - Clarence Esplanade, Portsmouth PO5 3PA.

Standard Parking

There are approximately 670 Portsmouth City Council owned off-street parking spaces, available in the city centre, each car park is clearly signed from the highway network. For information please click www.portsmouth.romanse.org.uk and click the parking tab on the right hand side.

MAP KEY:
- Park & Ride route - Portsmouth
- Park & Ride route - Cosham
- America's Cup World Series event stop
- Other Park & Ride stops (not ACWS)
- Event race village
- Walking route from Gunwharf Quays
- Walking route from city centre
- P Parking (strictly pre-booked only)
- E Arena entrances
- S Shuttle bus stop to arena

to Cosham park & ride

Portsmouth park & ride